EVERYTHING K-POP FANS SHOULD KNOW

Fascinating History, Iconic Idols, Fandom Culture, Record-Breaking Hits, and Much More!

SORA JUNG

Copyright 2025.

SPOTLIGHT MEDIA

ISBN: 978-1-951806-86-6

For questions, please reach out to:

Support@ActivityWizo.com

All Rights Reserved.

No part of this book may be reproduced or transmitted in any form or by any means, electronic or mechanical, including photocopying, recording, or by any other form without written permission from the publisher.

FREE BONUS

SCAN TO GET OUR NEXT BOOK FOR FREE!

TABLE OF CONTENTS

INTRODUCTION

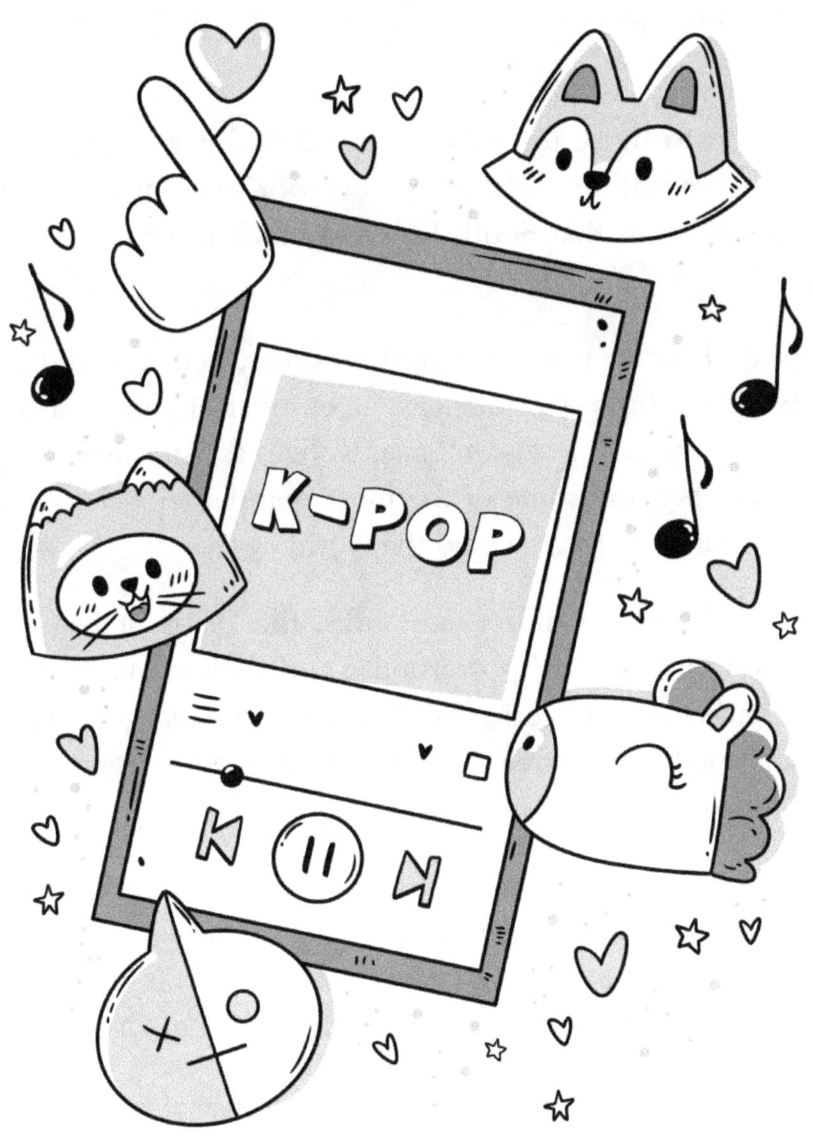

Millions of people around the world listen to K-pop. Statistics from the Korea Foundation suggests that nearly 100 million people belong to some sort of Korean cultural fan club, mostly related to K-pop and TV dramas. The majority of these fans are from Asia, but more than 25 million Americans and Europeans have joined fanbases.

In addition to those formally involved in fan groups, there are millions of casual fans. The magnitude of K-pop fans is especially astounding given that South Korea is home to under 52 million people.

K-pop, or Korean pop, is a South Korean genre of music that incorporates influences from a range of musical genres, including rap, R&B, dance, pop, and reggae. Korean artists, also known as idols, have become some of the most popular global superstars, with thousands of fans around the world.

Although the genre didn't exist until the 1990s, it has quickly developed into a global powerhouse and broken into the biggest music markets in the world. Its success has been largely facilitated by social media and streaming, which allowed the genre to gain worldwide exposure.

In this book, you'll enter the exciting — and sometimes confusing — world of K-pop to understand how it became what it is today. You'll learn all the fundamentals you need to become a fan (or better understand a loved one who's already a fan). You'll learn:

- What K-pop is and how it emerged as Korea became a highly developed nation and cultural hub
- Key terms, including fandom and Korean terms

- The story of K-pop's development through the generations and how it became a global force
- How music, choreography, and visuals come together to bring the music to life
- Fan behaviors and fandom etiquette
- How idols become idols and the structure of idol groups
- The broader culture of K-pop beyond the music
- How to begin your K-pop journey without getting overwhelmed

There's a lot to cover when it comes to K-pop, but there's never a boring moment for a K-pop fan. There's always more to learn, making K-pop a lifelong journey. By the time you finish this book, you'll be able to talk, think, and behave like a fan. Whether you want to fully immerse yourself in K-pop or you just want to learn to appreciate it, you're in the right place!

CHAPTER ONE: K-POP BASICS

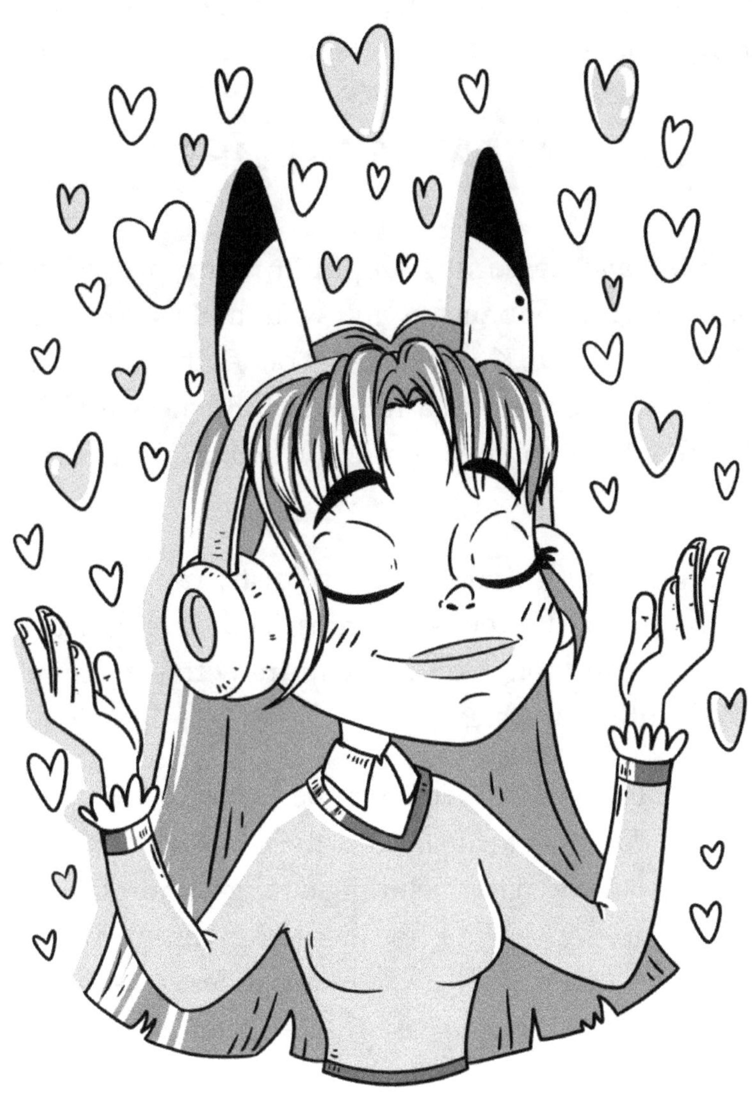

Over the past three decades, K-pop has developed from a fledgling genre into a global phenomenon, bringing a fresh, exciting sound into the pop sphere. This genre showcases not only vocal and rap talent, but also the role that dance and image have in taking music to the next level. The world of K-pop can seem daunting at first, but with just a bit of knowledge, you'll be ready to engage with all the fun and fandom that K-pop offers.

WHAT IS K-POP?

Most people have heard of K-pop, but many people don't fully understand what K-pop means and what makes it K-pop. Known as *gayo* in South Korea, K-pop has a lot of depth to it. It's more than just a genre. It incorporates a range of influences and brings the music to life with a unique training system that's used to develop talent.

Within K-pop, you'll find groups, soloists, rappers, and tons of interplay between different subgenres. Thus, K-pop isn't just one easily defined entity but a diverse culture with something to offer people with different tastes.

K-pop originated in South Korea in the 1990s and became popular in the early 2000s. There's no limit to the types of sounds it can use. In fact, K-pop is known for including a range of influences from all around the world, including traditional Korean music, R&B, pop, hip-hop, dance, and rock. With so many styles in use, pretty much anyone can find a K-pop artist that appeals to their particular tastes.

While music is at the heart of K-pop, it holds other notable attributes that distinguish it from other musical genres. K-pop often showcases dancing and visuals to add to its performances, and there's a structured industry to train and create its stars. One of the most important elements of K-pop is idol culture, which has created a subculture of fans who want to engage and connect with artists just as much as experiencing the music itself.

There's no doubt that K-pop is much more than just Korean pop music. This expansive culture strives to keep up with the pulse of its fans and global audiences, allowing people from around the world to share their passion and find joy in all K-pop has to offer. While K-pop has become a huge movement, it started with humble origins. Before it became the juggernaut it is today, it had to build itself up over decades of development.

THE HISTORY OF K-POP

Although K-pop is a relatively new genre of music, it's become one of the biggest cultural touchstones of this century. With its catchy beats, striking visuals, and ambitious productions, K-pop has established itself as a genre that defies expectations and continues to push its own limits.

The K-pop story begins with Seo Taiji and Boys in 1992 with the song "Nan Arayo (I Know)." Of course, Korean music existed long before this time, but much of it used traditional styles such as trot, which were viewed as old-fashioned by many young people. Seo Taiji and Boys brought hip-hop, dance, and R&B elements into their music. Young people in South Korea were excited to finally have music that was fresh, youthful, and distinctive from the music their parents listened to.

By 1996, the influence of Seo Taiji and the Boys had spread. The first recognized K-pop group, H.O.T., came out with the hit song "Candy," which uses elements of bubblegum pop. The group also took notes from J-pop and American boy bands. H.O.T. is notable for being created by SM Entertainment, one of South Korea's predominant entertainment companies, founded by Lee Soo-Man. It created a mold that would define how future groups and acts were formed.

Shortly after SM Entertainment, sometimes known as "SM Town," was founded, two other powerhouses emerged on the K-pop scene: JYP Entertainment, founded in 1997, and YG Entertainment, founded in 1998. JYP and YG went on to become SM's main competitors, with the three companies constantly competing to make stronger music.

SM Entertainment found success again in 1997 when girl group S.E.S. released "I'm Your Girl," inspired by Western girl groups like TLC. S.E.S. incorporated R&B elements that would go on to inspire the second generation of K-pop, which became known as the "Golden Age of K-Pop."

The late 2000s into the early 2010s was a powerful time for K-pop as the genre continued to evolve. In 2008, Rain broke through internationally with his song "Rainism." This song was notable for including English lyrics, which showcased the huge potential Korean artists had to appeal to a worldwide audience.

One of the major marks of K-pop's success during the second generation was its ability to break into the American market—the largest in the world—as well as other global markets, despite mostly being popular in East Asia in its early years. In 2009, Wonder Girls became the first Korean group to make the Billboard Hot 100 chart with the song "Nobody." SHINee's "Ring Ding Dong" highlighted an expansion of global influences by combining R&B with Euro-pop and autotuned vocals for a futuristic sound.

Artists and groups like Girls' Generation, IU, and 2NE1 continued to use global influences. That eventually led to the 2012 breakout hit "Gangnam Style," which brought PSY to the forefront of Western consciousness. At the end of the second generation, artists like BoA and BIGBANG continued to ease K-pop into the Western world with increasing amounts of English lyrics and Western pop influences.

By the time the third generation came along, K-pop was on a strong trajectory for increased global popularity. Groups like 2PM, GFRIEND, GOT7, TWICE, SEVENTEEN, Red Velvet, and EXO made names for themselves with diverse sounds. BLACKPINK became the biggest girl group on the planet, but no group made as big of a breakout as BTS.

Increased social media use and the availability of streaming platforms allowed groups to target global audiences more than ever before. Building on the work of their predecessors, third-generation groups established K-pop as a genre with creative concepts and constantly evolving styles.

Beginning in 2018, fourth-generation K-pop groups continued to benefit from the increased globalization of K-pop. Inspired by social media and virtual trends, concepts became even more innovative. Groups like Stray Kids, (G)I-DLE, ATEEZ, NewJeans, TOMORROW X TOGETHER, IVE, LE SSERAFIM, ENHYPEN, aespa, and ITZY have shown that K-pop can balance the demands of Korean audiences with those of increasing global audiences.

K-pop is now entering its fifth generation, and fans have yet to see the wonders this generation will bring; however, it's clear that artists will continue to work diligently, using the momentum of past generations to create music that appeals to fans around the world.

KEY K-POP TERMINOLOGY

What many people like about K-pop is its culture and community, which extend beyond the music into many areas of life. Not only does this culture impact how music is created and performed, but it also transforms the way fans engage with and enjoy the music. Because K-pop is about so much more than just the music itself, if you want to understand K-pop, you must understand the way it operates on several levels. To that end, you'll need to learn some key terms.

The sheer number of terms can seem overwhelming for new or casual fans, but each plays a role in how K-pop emerged as a predominant cultural movement of the late twentieth and early twenty-first centuries. Many of these terms will be explained more fully in later sections of this book, so don't worry if you can't fully grasp each one at first. You definitely don't need to memorize any terms, either; as you learn and experience K-pop, you'll start to naturally remember the terms. When in doubt, you can always use this section as your go-to K-pop dictionary.

You may notice that some of these terms are used more broadly in the music industry or fandom, while others are K-pop specific or based on Korean words. Some are also used differently in K-pop culture. While this list isn't exhaustive, it provides the chief terms you need. As with all language, these terms will evolve in response to new trends, so fans should constantly on the lookout for new terminology.

Note: Some of these definitions include other terms, but the list is alphabetical, so it should be easy to find the term you're looking for if it hasn't been defined yet!

Ace

Fans often refer to idols as *aces* when they display exceptional skill or talent.

Aegyo

Aegyo is a Korean term that describes cute behavior, and it can be seen throughout Korean culture. K-pop idols, both male and female, often adopt certain gestures, facial expressions, and voices to act cute for fans, showcasing their *aegyo*.

Akgae

Originating from a Korean term that means "malicious individual fan," the term *akgae* is used to describe fans who only like one member of a group and often insult their groupmates.

All-rounder

In K-pop, an *all-rounder* is someone who excels in any position. These idols show talent at vocals, visuals, dancing, and rap. *All-rounder* often describes individuals, but it can also be applied to groups as a whole.

Anti

An *anti*, also known as an *anti-fan*, is someone who doesn't like a specific idol or a group. Antis sometimes use aggressive or cruel behavior to show their dislike for an artist.

Bias

A *bias* is a person's favorite member of a group. Biases can change over time, and some people have multiple biases, sometimes within the same group.

Bias Wrecker

A *bias wrecker* refers to a person in a group who isn't a person's main bias but is still favored in some way. One's bias wrecker makes them tempted to change biases, and occasionally, a bias wrecker can become a bias.

Big Three

In K-pop, three companies have historically had the most successful acts: SM, JYP, and YG, collectively known as the "Big Three." HYBE, formerly known as Big Hit Entertainment, has challenged the Big Three due to its acquisition of BTS. HYBE is sometimes included with the Big Three as the Big Four, but HYBE is still relatively new in its prominence.

Black Ocean

A *black ocean* occurs when fans in a crowd turn off their light sticks to show disapproval for a performer, mostly at performances including multiple acts. It can be related to fan disputes or a fandom's displeasure with what their biased group is doing.

B-side

A B-side is any song on an album other than the main track.

Bubble

Bubble refers to any of the paid apps that idols use to send messages to fans. You can also send messages to an idol on these platforms. Idols send the same messages to all subscribers of their bubble but often personalize them by using a Y/N ("your name") feature that automatically inserts each user's name.

Center

The *center* of a group is featured over other members in music videos, performances, and photo shoots. This member usually has strong visuals, is highly popular, or has strong dancing skills.

Comeback

Comeback refers to a group's new release. Comebacks include new music, promotional material, and shows. They're incredibly grueling for artists, with intense schedules and tons of prep before the comeback even happens.

Comeback Stage

The term *comeback stage* is used to describe the performance where an artist presents their new song on a music show. These performances set the tone for how the comeback will go and express the concept of the comeback.

Concept

In K-pop, a *concept* is the theme a group uses during a comeback. This concept will be seen throughout the songs, style, photos, and promos used during that era. Many groups start out with a sweet, innocent concept and move on to more mature themes as their careers evolve.

Daesang

A *daesang* (literally "grand prize") award is one of the highest honors artists and groups can receive in Korean music.

Debut

Just as in the broader music industry, an artist's debut is their initial release. This may be either a song or an album.

Ending Fairy

The *ending fairy* refers to the end of a K-pop stage, where performers strike a memorable or visually appealing pose. The ending fairy is determined by the cameraman, usually focusing on the visual of a member or, occasionally, multiple members.

Face of the Group

The *Face of the Group* is the member who garners the most public attention. This member is often perceived as the group's representative. They may also be a *visual*, but that's not always the case. While visuals are chosen based on looks, the Face of the Group is determined by popularity.

Fanbase

Fanbases are organized pages or sites dedicated to helping their idols through different supportive behaviors. They organize fans using various strategies, including translating, social media, voting, streaming, and fundraising. Some fanbases are specific to a certain country, while others focus on a particular aspect of fandom, like an idol's fashion.

Fancams

In general, *fancams* are amateur videos fans take of their biases, but fancams have extra meaning in K-pop. Originally, fans used these to spread performances that would otherwise not have been broadcasted. These days, broadcasters often post fancams to showcase individual members or moments that weren't shown on the main camera. These videos allow fans access to footage of their bias during the entire performance. Fancams are often shot vertically to better show choreography, but *facecams* are usually shot horizontally to showcase the idol's face.

Fansign

A *fansign* is an event where, through buying merchandise, fans can earn entries to meet or interact with idols.

Fansite

A *fansite* is someone who goes to events, airports, and concerts to take high-quality photos of their idols, usually with professional-grade equipment.

Fan Café

The term *fan café* refers to Korean web forums, usually hosted on Naver Café or Daum Café. Some companies have official fan cafés, while others use alternate platforms to share official information and engage with fanbases.

Fan Calls

Fan calls were created during the COVID-19 pandemic to replace fansigns since in-person meetings weren't possible. These are essentially short video calls with idols. Fans enter to win fan calls by buying merchandise online, often buying more of a designated purchase to earn multiple entries.

Fan Chant

A *fan chant* is a prearranged chant, usually coordinated by fanbases or fan clubs, that fans use when idols perform. These chants are recited at designated times and can be anything from certain lyrics or phrases to simply the names of band members. These chants keep fans involved and are a tradition that helps maintain a high energy during performances.

Fan Club

A *fan club* is a group of fans who organize to support an idol or idol group. Fan clubs may be officially created by entertainment companies, but fans also frequently form non-official clubs.

Fan Service

Fan service is any behavior idols perform specifically to appeal to fans. Fan service includes a range of actions, such as *skinship* and fan interactions, but really, it involves anything the idol does, knowing it will please their fans.

Fan Wars

Fan wars are feuds, fights, or other disagreements between fans of competing groups. These interactions typically take place on social media.

Finger Heart

A *finger heart* is a common gesture used in K-pop where the thumb and index finger are crossed to make the shape of a heart.

Generation

K-pop currently has five generations, the first of which began in the 1990s. Groups or soloists are placed in a generation based on when they debut. The generation of an idol or group impacts their sound, choreography, style, concepts, and even fan trends.

Hallyu

The term *Hallyu*, or "Korean Wave," was coined to describe the increasing popularity of South Korean culture throughout the world due to music, TV, and other media.

Hanbok

Hanbok is a type of traditional clothing worn in South Korea that K-pop artists occasionally wear for music videos or photo shoots.

Hi-touch

Hi-touch is a type of fan engagement in K-pop where fans touch hands with idols after a concert or other events using gestures like high fives or handshakes.

Hoobae

A *hoobae* is a less-experienced artist or group. A *hoobae* is determined not by age but by debut date.

Hwaiting

In K-pop, *Hwaiting* is a way to cheer people on, particularly idols. The term derives from the English word *fighting*, which can also be seen in K-pop.

Idol Group

An *idol group* is a K-pop group with two or more members, each of whom has a specific place and role. Groups can be quite large — even over 20 members — but most have between four and nine members.

It Boy or It Girl

The term *It Boy* or *It Girl* is used to describe a K-pop artist who is one of the top idols of their generation.

Khia

Khia is a word used among fans to express that people don't care or know about a person or group.

Koreaboo

Koreaboo is a derisive term used to describe a non-Korean person who is obsessed with Korean culture. Koreaboos regularly fetishize Korean culture rather than genuinely appreciating and understanding the nuances of Korean life.

Lightstick

As their name suggests, *lightsticks* are sticks that have a light at the top. Each group or artist has their own official light stick with different designs and colors. Light sticks are used the most at events like concerts that have audiences.

Line

The term *lines* refers to different idols who share a common quality or role. The vocalists in a group may be called the *vocal line,* while the dancers form the *dancer line.* Fans can get incredibly creative when naming and inventing lines for their idols.

Liners

Liners are the members who make up a K-pop line. For example, idols born in the year 2000 may be called *'00 liners.* Fans sometimes identify themselves in this same way to find fans of similar ages.

Locals

The term *local* is used to refer to people outside the K-pop fandom — basically, anyone who doesn't like K-pop.

Maknae

The *maknae* is the youngest member of a group.

Ment

Ment, short for *comment,* refers to the time when idols speak to the audience.

Mini-album

K-pop groups usually refer to extended play (EP) albums as *mini albums*. These albums are shorter than full-length albums and usually have five to seven songs.

Multi

The shortened term *multi* is often used to describe multi-stans, who are fans of multiple groups.

Music Show

Music shows are an essential part of K-pop. These programs are broadcast weekly with different artists performing during comeback promos. Korea's main broadcasters each have their own show. Popular shows include *Music Bank*, *Inkigayo*, *M Countdown*, *Music Core*, *Show Champion*, and *The Show*. They rank songs according to different scoring systems using factors like streaming, album sales, pre-voting, live voting, social media, video, and broadcast.

Netizen

A *netizen* is someone who uses the internet or is part of an internet community, and in K-pop, this term is used to describe primarily online fans. For instance, Korean fans may be called *K-nets*. The word *netizen* shouldn't be mistaken for *NCTzen*, which is a fan of the group NCT.

Nugu

Nugu comes from the Korean word meaning "who." It's used to describe relatively unknown groups or artists because, upon hearing their name, someone might ask, "Who?"

OST

OST is short for "original soundtrack." Many K-pop artists create OSTs for different pieces of media, but these are generally not allowed to compete on music shows.

OTP

OTP stands for "one true pairing," a term often used in fandom by *shippers* who support or fantasize about a relationship between K-pop artists.

Perfect All-kill

A *perfect all-kill* (PAK) is an achievement in which an artist ranks number one on all the Korean music charts (real time, daily, and weekly) simultaneously.

Photocard

Photocards are collectible pictures of idols' faces that are about the size of a debit card. They're often included with albums or other merchandise. Sometimes, though, they're sold on their own. They're a lot like trading cards. Most of the time, photocards are included at random, so fans try to collect their desired photocards by buying more albums or trading with other fans.

Positions

Each member of a group is given a *position*, often determined by the group's company. However, not all groups have official positions. The five essential positions are leader, vocalist, dancer, rapper, and visual, but groups may also include a center, the Face of the Group, and the *maknae*. In larger groups, some of these positions are broken down further as main, lead, and sub.

Saranghae

Saranghae means "I love you" in Korean.

Sasaeng

Sasaeng is a term used to describe a fan who is overly obsessed. These fans often stalk idols or break their personal boundaries.

Selca

Selca is a portmanteau of the English words *self* and *camera*. Basically, it's an alternate term for *selfie* — though the Korean term was actually invented first! Idols often share selcas with fans to help create a deeper connection.

Skinship

Skinship refers to physical affection between idols, be it romantic, platonic, or familial. Fans often like when idols show skinship.

Solo Stan

A *solo stan* is a person who only likes one member from a group. It's important to note that solo stans aren't actively hateful like *akgaes* are.

Stan

The word *stan* stems from the song of the same name by Eminem, which describes an obsessive fan. In K-pop, it's used lightheartedly to refer to fans who're incredibly devoted to a specific artist or group. Though this word can be used derisively, fans often use it proudly.

Stan Attractor

A *stan attractor* is an idol who draws attention from non-fans and makes them interested in the group. Usually, stan attractors have special features such as good looks or an amiable personality.

Subunit

As its name suggests, a *subunit* is a smaller group of members who work together on projects outside of full-group activities.

Sunbae

Sunbae is a Korean term that younger artists use when addressing seniors. For idols, seniority is determined based on an idol's debut date rather than their age.

Survival Show

A *survival show* is one avenue many trainees go through before debuting in a group. Trainees participate in these competitions in the hopes of gaining a position in a group set to debut. Additionally, they give groups the chance to build a fanbase before even releasing their first song.

Title Track

While you may think the *title track* always shares the same name as the album it's featured on, that's not always the case. In K-pop, a title track leads the album, usually accompanied by a music video. This is a song selected by the group, soloist, or company to receive the most promotion during a comeback. The title track is designed for comeback stages and music shows, often representing the tone and concept of the entire album.

Trainee

Before a K-pop idol debuts, they generally must go through the training process. *Trainees* are taught the essential skills K-pop idols need, such as dancing, singing, and rapping. Trainees can start their training as young as 10 years old, but most are teenagers. Trainees may train for months or even years before debuting.

Ult

The term *ult* — short for *ultimate* — is generally used to describe a person's number one favorite bias among all groups and idols. It can also apply to a person's top group if they bias multiple groups.

This term may be attached to others, such as *ult bias wrecker* or *ult song*.

Ulzzang

The Korean word *ulzzang* means "best face" or "good-looking." It's used to describe someone who has become popular on the internet because they have distinctive visuals.

Visual

Visual refers to an idol who's recognized for their striking appearance, usually the idol in a group who most conforms to Korean beauty standards. This role is often assigned by agencies, but not all groups have an officially designated visual. Visuals are often featured in music videos, magazine shoots, or group photos.

V-live

V-live was a video streaming service used to connect idols and fans that has since merged with Weverse before shutting down in 2022. While V-live is no longer active, it's still mentioned in fandom spaces, particularly in discussions involving groups who were active from 2015 to 2022.

HOW K-POP IDOLS ARE TRAINED

One of the most notable aspects of K-pop is its unique training system. K-pop idols obtain some of the most extensive training of any artists in the world. During this training, idols-to-be learn and compete in hopes of eventually getting to debut in a group. The trainee process can be grueling, but many trainees consider it to be more than worth it.

In the Korean music development system, the process starts with training and development, known as T&D. T&D allows companies to search for individuals with promise and teach them the skills they'll need to someday debut as a soloist or in a group.

Before trainees even start learning the tricks of the trade, they must be scouted. Each company has its own team tasked with identifying and bringing in talent through auditions, street searches, or social media. Talent development teams don't just focus on current abilities but primarily look for potential. Most skills can be taught, so companies focus on the elusive "it factor."

Once recruited, trainees undergo rigorous classes to develop their skills as efficiently as possible. This training is all-consuming, and most idols devote themselves completely to their training. During training—and even after they debut—idols often live in company dorms, but some go home to sleep if they live nearby. Being a trainee is like having a job for K-pop hopefuls.

The goal trainees share is to improve their skills so that they can meet or exceed basic requirements for debuting. The company funds the required training in hopes that they'll get a return on their investment. Trainees' progress is monitored by their company to make sure they keep up with the demands of a K-pop idol, and if trainees don't make sufficient progress, they may be cut.

THE STRUCTURE OF K-POP GROUPS

Over the years, K-pop groups have evolved to have a very specific structure. Earlier groups were still working on finding the right formula, so they don't align perfectly with the structure of newer K-pop groups. However, their influence shaped the priorities and roles group members are expected to conform to.

The roles within the group are strategically assigned to best fit their desired audience's preferences. The idea is for each member to focus on a specific aspect so that the audience can easily identify different members without having to spend much time in research. Ideally, each member will possess unique qualities that cover any weaknesses among the rest of the group.

Of course, each group handles positions a little differently, as it's nearly impossible for every idol to perfectly conform to these categories. K-pop groups tend to be relatively large, so multiple members are sometimes assigned to the same position. Roles can also evolve over time as certain members develop skills outside their assigned roles. While sometimes complex, assigned positions give fans a general idea of each idol's strengths.

Leader

The leader of a K-pop group is generally the idol who takes care of other members and leads in various situations. Group leaders may be the oldest member of the group, but they might be chosen for other reasons, such as having trained for the longest or possessing the best overall leadership qualities. Not all groups have an assigned leader, but those that do usually only have one.

Maknae

As previously discussed, the maknae is the youngest member. This person can impact the group's overall dynamics, so their role is far from trivial. The maknae is often cute, serving as a symbol of innocence; however, the role has evolved over time, and *maknaes* are now expected to represent the evolution and growth of the group as a whole. *Maknaes* are doted on, and due to their youthful energy, often bring balance by keeping the group invigorated and playful. Thus, the ability of the maknae to encourage harmony and inspire energy is vital for any K-pop group.

Examples of prominent *maknaes* include:

- Jungkook from BTS
- BLACKPINK's Lisa
- Stray Kids' I.N.
- EXO's Sehun
- SHINee's Taemin
- Red Velvet's Yeri
- ENHYPEN's Ni-Ki
- ATEEZ's Jongho
- aespa's Ningning
- TXT's Huening Kai

Face of the Group

The Face of the Group is usually the member that is best known by the public. They're often good looking but don't necessarily serve as the visual. The Face of the Group serves as the group's representative but isn't formally assigned. Some groups don't have a Face of the Group, and because of this, fans may debate who the "real" Face of the Group is.

Vocalist

Vocalists are responsible for the bulk of singing within a group. Most groups will include all members in vocals to some extent, but the strongest singers will be assigned the vocal role in the group.

Vocalists are split into three categories:

Main: As you might expect, the main vocalist possesses the best vocal skills and strongest technique, so they handle the harder vocal parts.

Lead: Lead vocalists have the second-strongest vocal abilities. They're called the lead because their parts often lead into the main vocalist's parts.

Sub: Sub vocalists (or simply vocalists) still sing, but they don't get as many lines and are often relegated to harmonies.

Dancer

All members of a group dance, but each has a different role based on their abilities.

Main: The main dancer is the most skilled and is generally featured in the choreography. They're often given solos, along with central positions in dances.

Lead: The lead dancer is the second-best dancer, often dancing in a prominent position. They may sometimes get solos.

Rapper

The rappers of the group are responsible for the rapping parts of a song. Many members may have rap parts, but not all members need strong rapping skills.

Main: The main rapper gets the most parts because of their skill. Rappers sometimes write their own lyrics, but that's not always the case, especially in groups that have less of a focus on rap.

Lead: Lead rappers are the second-best rappers of the group, and their raps usually lead into the main rapper's parts.

Sub: Sub rappers are given limited parts, but they do rap, unlike non-rapping members.

Visual

As you already know, a visual is the group member who's considered the most attractive based on Korean beauty standards. Some praiseworthy traits in Korean culture include:

- Double eyelids
- Large eyes
- Pale, clear skin
- A high nose bridge
- Thin (particularly for women)
- Small, V-shaped face
- Tall (particularly for men)

As attitudes toward beauty evolve, it's possible for idols to defy some of these standards, but they still dominate the industry. For example, idols with darker skin tones are often whitewashed in content to make their skin fit more with the beauty standard.

Some idols go to extreme lengths, sticking to harsh diets or having surgery in an effort to meet these expectations. Thus, it will be interesting to see how the role of visuals evolves over the coming years.

Center

The center, generally the Face of the Group or a visual, is the group member who tends to stand in the middle during promotions, music videos, or photo shoots. However, different promotions often have different centers.

CHAPTER TWO:
THE EVOLUTION OF K-POP

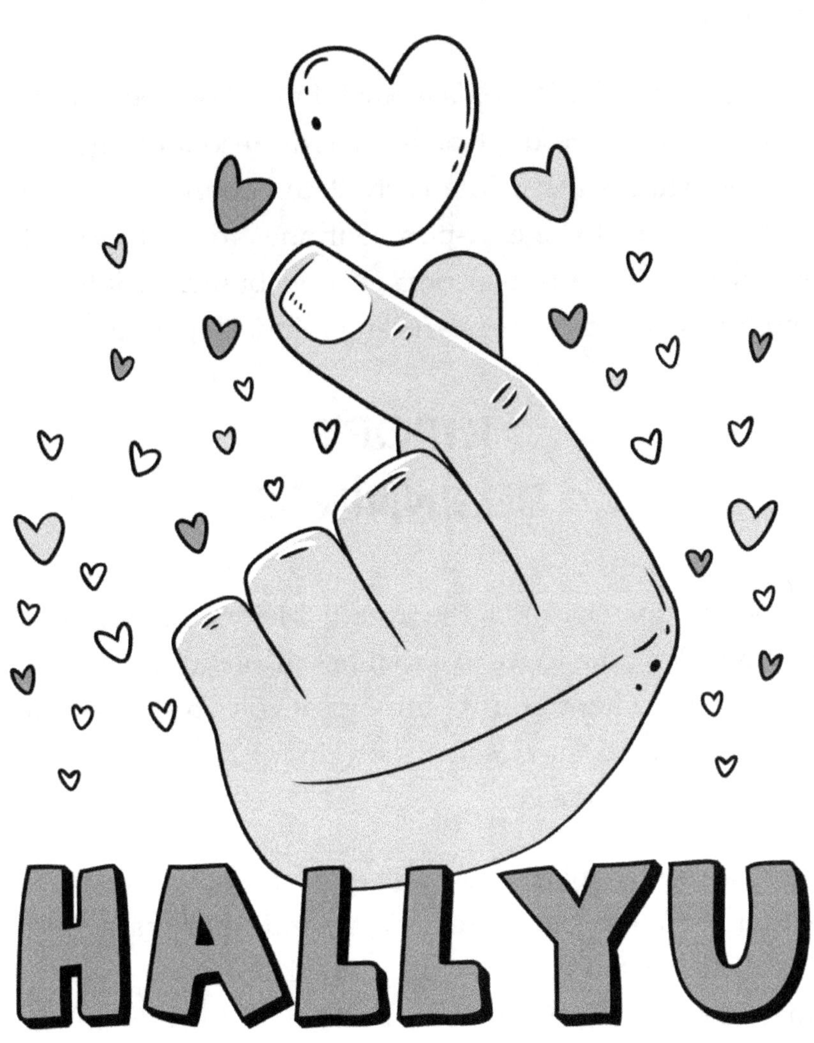

From humble origins, K-pop has proven to be a lasting influence on global pop culture and a mechanism of Korean soft power — the ability of a country to have international influence through co-opting rather than coercion. K-pop's story shows how the Korean government's deliberate investment in cultural opportunities has created an environment that spreads influence through fan development.

In just a few decades, K-pop's growth has surpassed expectations, interconnected with South Korea's massive economic growth from an impoverished state in the early 20th century to a prominent actor on the global stage. K-pop continues to evolve, celebrating the strength and pride of Korea. K-pop branches into areas far beyond music and into the hearts and minds of people worldwide.

K-POP'S BEGINNINGS

Now that you've learned the rough history of K-pop and its generations, it's time to learn about how Korean history impacted K-pop's development and its important role in the country. The 1990s is considered the decade of origin for K-pop as a genre, but its roots start much earlier.

In many ways, K-pop's story begins in the 1950s, a time of transition through the Korean War and the post-war period. During this time, musicians like the Kim Sisters showed the promise of cultural power. They performed for U.S. soldiers and even appeared on the *Ed Sullivan Show* 22 times. The Kim Sisters' success foreshadowed the musical domination in the decades ahead; however, first, South Korea had to build its struggling economy to gain sufficient resources to promote its talent around the world.

During the 1950s, South Korea was a predominantly agrarian society. North Korea held most of the electrical and industrial power, so South Korea suffered huge economic hardships post-war. The country had to make careful decisions if it wanted to grow in the second half of the twentieth century.

The 1960s saw South Korea operating under a military government. In the three decades of military rule, economic advancement became known as the "miracle on the Han," a reference to the river that runs through Seoul. South Korea became focused on modernization through increased education, industry, and infrastructure. Companies like Samsung would become a foundation of South Korea's modern economy, enabling economic growth no one could have anticipated.

Music was an important part Korean life at this time, but many popular singers and songs were banned by the government under military rule. Combined with a corrupt music industry, artists struggled to thrive.

By the 1970s, South Korea had established plans for economic growth—and these efforts paid off. Economic improvement allowed the South Korean public to become more socially aware, leading to a pro-democracy movement. Musicians like Kim Minki expressed political dissonance through their music, and though his music was ultimately banned, his activism encouraged the youth. He established music as not merely entertainment but a vessel for societal change.

Thanks to the pro-democracy movement, South Korea held its first free presidential election in 1987. By that point, the government had relaxed censorship, enabling citizens—including musicians—to express themselves more freely. During this time, artists like Park Namjung, Kim Wansun, and Sobangcha demonstrated the promise of Korean music. Increased freedoms, economic development, and music's growing influence on South Korean society ushered in the 1990s, creating a foundation for K-pop's first generation.

During the late 1980s and early 1990s, most of South Korea's youth enjoyed listening to Western music, feeling that Korean music was mostly for their parents. However, that all changed when Seo Taiji and Boys performed on TV in 1992. The group offered a radical and exciting alternative to South Korean music, which was often viewed as old and stuffy. The new music didn't sound like traditional music and had diverse Western influences. It was something the new generation could be proud of.

Because South Korea had become freer over the preceding decades, although many people resisted the new music, censorship no longer prevented countercultural music from becoming popular. From that moment, the South Korean music industry had all it needed for rapid growth. The government of South Korea, instead of resisting the musical movements, began to invest millions of dollars into K-pop, creating the *Hallyu*.

THE HALLYU: SPREADING K-POP WORLDWIDE

K-pop's emergence as a global cultural phenomenon is often called the Korean Wave, also known as *Hallyu*. This refers to the spread of Korean culture over the past few decades through music, TV, cinema, fashion, and more. K-pop became not just something enjoyed by South Koreans but something that global audiences cherish.

The global market for K-pop emerged throughout the 1990s as entertainment companies like SM, JYP, and YG gained footing by creating new acts modeled on early successes. These companies achieved monumental success with popular groups like Girls' Generation, Super Junior, f(x), SHINee, and TVXQ. These groups used mixed-language lyrics and collaborations to promote their music.

Other Asian markets like China and Taiwan also enjoyed modest successes during the 1990s. Some groups set their sights on the large Japanese market, but for the most part, early K-pop was marketed primarily within South Korea. Soon, though, the tide turned, and companies began purposefully creating content geared toward international audiences.

The Asian Financial Crisis of 1997 spurred additional changes in South Korea as much of the population struggled financially, and fledgling companies struggled to stay afloat. Countries all across Asia were impacted by the crisis, but South Korea, the Philippines, Thailand, Malaysia, and Indonesia were among the most affected.

This put South Korean companies in a difficult position, and the answer for many sectors was to go global.

The big entertainment companies tried to determine what markets would be optimal; the natural first choice was the coveted Japanese music market, the second-largest in the world next to the United States. Japan made strategic sense because it was a neighboring East Asian region. Despite lingering tensions spurred by Japan's occupation of Korea, conquering the Japanese market became South Korean entertainment's new mission.

The early 2000s offered tons of promise to enter the Japanese market. SM's BoA debuted in 2000, and her career was designed to break into Japan. This move encouraged K-pop acts to learn Japanese so that they could capitalize on the market. In 2002, Korea and Japan hosted the FIFA World Cup, which exposed huge Japanese and international audiences to K-pop. Artists like BoA were able to top the charts even outside of Japan, leading companies to put additional resources into Japanese markets.

K-pop companies weren't satisfied with just influence in Japan, though; their dream was to break into American markets too. SM made this clear by creating a slogan for BoA: "Best of Asia, Bring on America." At this time, BoA enjoyed some success in America, becoming the first South Korean to chart on the Billboard 200. However, most of America still didn't know K-pop even existed.

From the early days of K-pop, select pockets of American K-pop fans existed. The U.S. is home to the largest population of diasporic Koreans, mostly in California, New York, and New Jersey. Los Angeles and New York City were hotspots for Korean Americans. Events like the Korean Music Festival proved there was a U.S.

audience for K-pop, and in 2003, it became the first multi-artist concert to sell out the Hollywood Bowl. However, beyond the Korean American community, there was limited interest in K-pop.

Progress during this era may have been slow, but it was important. Rain likely had the most success of early artists. In 2006, he was named as one of *Time*'s 100 Most Influential People and sold out two shows at Madison Square Garden, but he received mixed reviews. He continued his attempts to reach American audiences, but before he could build momentum, he had to report for mandatory military service in 2011. YG Entertainment also held three U.S. shows in 2006 for three of their artists: 1TYM, Se7en, and BIGBANG. Powerhouse domestic artists like BoA and Rain even released English singles to capture the attention of American audiences, but these efforts ultimately fell flat.

As the first decade of the twenty-first century drew to a close, JYP's Wonder Girls showed, yet again, the potential of K-pop groups in America with the 2009 release of "Nobody" in English. They became the first K-pop group to reach the Billboard Hot 100 and even opened for the Jonas Brothers.

However, after Sunmi left the group, their momentum slowed. Despite releasing additional English singles and embarking on a North American tour, the Wonder Girls never broke through. By 2012, they went on hiatus, scrapping their English album.

Through the 2000s and 2010s, plenty of acts attempted to win over foreign audiences, but despite success in Asian markets, even Korea's biggest superstars were unable to achieve widespread success—or even recognition—from most Americans. That all changed with the advent of social media, which allowed people to engage with music and artists in new ways; this enabled K-pop to make waves beyond Asia and finally enter new global markets.

THE ROLE OF SOCIAL MEDIA & STREAMING IN K-POP'S GROWTH

When K-pop was created, people still discovered and listened to music through using CDs, radios, and TV shows. However, shortly afterward, technology began to shake up the music industry. Two major innovations forever changed how people listen to and interact with music: social media and streaming. These two new technologies allowed new audiences to find K-pop and platform the fandoms that made K-pop not just music but a movement.

The Power of Streaming

The momentum of K-pop in the West isn't limited to social media. Another huge factor is the shift in how people listened to music. Before streaming, most people either bought music or listened to the radio, limiting how much and what kind of music they could listen to. As a result, Western audiences had minimal access to K-pop. However, the rise of streaming exposed new audiences to the genre.

Throughout the 1990s, MP3 technology made it easier to engage with all types of genres. In 1999, the music-sharing website Napster offered new ways to download and share music, including rare recordings that listeners couldn't otherwise access. Eventually, Napster was shut down, but it highlighted the demand for digital music—and companies took notice.

Piracy allowed people to share digital files, but these files commonly came with viruses and were a hassle to download. However, in 2003, the creation of iTunes offered an alternative, making it possible to legally buy digital music easily and efficiently. As a result, people invested in technologies like MP3 players, which already existed but hadn't yet surpassed the popularity of CDs.

The continued evolution of music-sharing platforms and their associated technology encouraged people to buy digital music. This trend made it easier to listen to diverse and harder-to-find music. Fans no longer had to hunt down K-pop CDs, which weren't always easy to find, especially in areas without a large Korean-American population.

Access became even easier when Pandora created its online streaming service, which played new music for customers and suggested songs based on their listening history. This allowed people to hear new music without having to either buy or borrow it. Eventually, services like Spotify and Apple Music created their own streaming platforms, providing users with access to music from all around the world.

The advent of streaming platforms made it easy to introduce potential fans to new music and get them hooked. In today's fan culture, streaming is a vital part of any comeback, and fans work hard to get idols as many streams as possible.

Fandom Through Social Media

The success of K-pop as a global genre relies on one key factor: fandom. While entertainment companies tried to push idols beyond the Asian market, they faced many obstacles; the greatest of these was the fact that average global consumers didn't even know about K-pop and had few opportunities to learn about it.

Most foreign audiences had little reason to give K-pop a try. Yes, some artists and songs received minimal attention, but Korean artists struggled to build reliable global fanbases. However, K-pop clearly had potential, and in the late 2000s and 2010s, the second and third generation of K-pop gained access to a pivotal advantage: social media.

K-pop companies began to bring their content to social media platforms like Twitter, Facebook, and YouTube. Since these platforms had international user interfaces, they could connect consumers to global content in unprecedented ways.

New audiences could share information through social media campaigns and create organic growth. The Korean government even sponsored initiatives to embrace emerging technology and make pop culture a priority for Korea's international relations. This process included networking, marketing, and market research.

K-pop marketing included music videos with catchy songs and eye-catching visuals, and live performances with strong choreography made K-pop even more appealing. Songwriters also began including more English lyrics in the songs. Netizens could stumble on K-pop and easily get drawn in, even if they had no prior knowledge of the genre.

Social media allowed artists to gain larger audiences, but fans did their part as well by bridging language and cultural gaps. Fans took the initiative to translate content, which helped people not only to engage with the music but also learn who the idols were as individuals and groups. Fans no longer had to understand Korean to engage with live streams, social media posts, interviews, and other content. Consequently, Western audiences became more excited and involved in K-pop.

In many ways, fans were K-pop's main promoters, freely investing their time and energy in projects to benefit their idols. Things like blogs, social media posts, and fan videos added a new level of accessibility and engagement for international fans. Idols used these websites to connect with fans to create a sense of immediacy and community. Thus, fans weren't limited to a distant connection to their idols but felt as though they were an integral part of their idols' journeys.

YouTube was one of the biggest platforms for early social media success in K-pop. Several music videos, particularly from SM groups, went viral, including SHINee's "Ring Ding Dong," Girls' Generation's "Gee," TVXQ's "Mirotic," Super Junior's "Sorry, Sorry," and f(x)'s "Electric Shock." This success was due to SM's strategy of SM Town, which treated groups and idols like a big family under the SM name. The company also encouraged collaborations in hopes of uniting the power of fandoms. SM made efforts to use social media, but it was YG Entertainment that had the biggest breakthrough in the second generation.

YG had several successes of its own, including several hits from BIGBANG, whose hits continued to influence the industry in subsequent generations. Meanwhile, 2NE1 displayed the potential of girl groups to make a splash online. These YG artists gained strong streaming numbers on YouTube, but no YG artist would influence Western domination quite as much as PSY, who made the most viral Western breakthrough of his generation.

In 2012, PSY's uber-catchy "Gangnam Style" became a viral hit, earning play on American radios after gaining traction on YouTube. It was so popular that it became the first YouTube song to reach one billion views and remains one of the most popular songs ever on the platform with over four billion views. "Gangnam Style" reached number two on the Billboard Hot 100 chart, with about five million sales in the U.S. alone. In South Korea, PSY earned the 4th Class Order of Cultural Merit from the Ministry of Culture, Sports, and Tourism. Then, President Obama suggested that the song was bringing people around the globe into the Korean Wave.

PSY's Western success transformed K-pop, not just in its global success but also in how it was treated domestically. The spotlight was now on the third generation of K-pop, which came with additional pressure for aspiring young idols. K-pop had become a source of national pride, and idols were held to higher standards than ever.

As K-pop gained international popularity, the demand for young talent in Korea grew, and the role of social media became even more important. Third-generation groups began to increase their presence on social media and promote more online interaction with fans.

In 2015, JYP's girl group TWICE started an Instagram account, gaining thousands of followers within two hours. Companies began to audition for talent in global locations, including Japan, Thailand, Canada, the U.S., and Australia, in hopes of attracting more international fans. Broadcasters put on survival shows to create groups through TV competitions, which created fans on social media before groups even debuted.

The third generation marked an era in which groups gained success by appealing to young people on social media spaces. Groups like TWICE, NCT, iKON, BLACKPINK, WINNER, MONSTA X, PENTAGON, SEVENTEEN, GFRIEND, ASTRO, SF9, and EXO all showcase the third generation's ability to create fandoms and find international support through social media. Even so, no group from the third generation is as well known as BTS, who earned themselves a bigger global audience than any other group.

BTS & THE GLOBAL PHENOMENON

If there's any K-pop group that even non-fans know about, it's BTS. No one could have predicted how big BTS would become. The group's success was so unprecedented, and they didn't even come from one of the Big Three! At the time, BTS's company, Big Hit Entertainment, was small and relatively unknown.

In 2013, BTS—short for *Bangtan Sonyeondan* ("Bulletproof Boy Scouts")—debuted with the single "2 Cool 4 School." The group's album spoke to K-pop's roots, using influences from 1990s K-pop groups and discussing societal issues in Korea. The initial concept excited fans, and BTS transformed with each new concept, showcasing the group's growth and development. The group honed their sound, earning their first *daesang* after their 2015 comeback.

Big Hit's CEO, Bang Sihyuk, wanted the group to not only have a great discography but also to introduce a "BTS universe." The idea was to use visuals and storytelling to incorporate references, hidden messages, and societal commentary that was unlike many other groups of the time. Most idols had to maintain a specific image, and while BTS members still had roles, the group appealed to many fans who saw them as more open and real. It was that openness that allowed BTS to finally win over the long-coveted American market.

In 2017, BTS introduced the compilation *Love Yourself*, which told a story of self-love and addressed important issues young people face. The release was later associated with UNICEF's *Love Myself* initiative to tackle violence and bullying. In 2018, the group's leader, Kim Namjoon, was even asked to give a speech at the United Nations. This global recognition led the group to become the first K-pop group to win Billboard Music Awards Top Social Artist. The group also performed "DNA," their first Billboard Hot 100 entry, at the American Music Awards.

In 2018, the group's success continued to grow, no doubt thanks to the massive growth of their fanbase and support on social media. BTS released the first K-pop album to reach #1 on the Billboard 200 chart for their debut week, eventually earning the genre's first platinum certification from the Recording Industry Association of America.

The members performed "Fake Love" at the Billboard Music Awards, another huge opportunity to reach American audiences.

They also appeared at the Grammy Awards and headlined a global stadium tour. The group broke record after record, demonstrating that K-pop groups could enter the mainstream global consciousness.

Over the years, BTS continued working to prove themselves as one of the most popular musical groups in the world. In the early 2020s, despite challenges presented by the COVID-19 pandemic, the group kept in touch with fans through virtual events and livestreams. In 2020, BTS received their first Grammy nomination and set a record as the group with the most Billboard Music Awards of all time. They enjoyed similar success at home, earning more *daesangs* than any other South Korean artist.

Despite success in the West, BTS struggled with racism and hateful comments. Many Americans still didn't understand or like BTS, but the group was undeniably successful, especially after English hits like "Dynamite," "Butter," and "Permission to Dance" entered the charts. Members kept pushing themselves, and their fans supported them at every chance.

BTS showed other groups that K-pop idols could become global icons as well. In fact, BTS ushered in an era where many groups had more international fans than domestic fans. Fourth-generation groups had big shoes to fill, but they could also venture into new pursuits and take advantage of opportunities made possible by the boom of K-pop popularity.

K-POP'S INFLUENCE ON FASHION & BEAUTY

Consumers around the world are inspired by the style and looks of K-pop idols. Other Asians and Westerners have started to emulate trends showcased by Korean idols. This shift is exciting for many Koreans, who take pride in the spread of their culture, but there are also concerns related to cultural appropriation that fans should consider while exploring Korean fashion and beauty trends.

KOREAN BEAUTY STANDARDS

As we've already covered, certain physical traits are highly valued and expected from K-pop artists. These include pale skin, a slim build, big eyes, and an overall youthful look. Women are encouraged to look almost like porcelain dolls. Men have fewer pressures but are still required to abide by certain standards. Many men spend a lot of time on skincare, and it's not uncommon for them to wear light makeup on a regular basis.

WEST MEETS EAST: THE SPREAD OF EAST ASIAN TRENDS

Although many Asian trends have been historically slow to catch on in the West, fashion, and beauty trends have started to pique the interest of many Westerners, particularly young people interested in K-pop and Korean culture. From skincare to fashion, Korea influences trends around the world and will likely continue to impact how people express themselves through outward appearance.

Of all the Korean trends Westerners have adopted, perhaps the most notable is skincare, which is considered a huge priority. Koreans prefer perfect skin over the use of makeup. As a result, extensive skincare regimes are common. While some adopt a relatively short three-step routine, it's normal for many Koreans to have seven to twelve steps in their daily regimen. While this might seem excessive, it speaks to the Korean idea that, before putting on makeup, it's crucial to prepare a strong foundation. Men and women alike appreciate the power of keeping their skin healthy and their looks closest to the Korean ideal.

When exploring personal style, many fans turn to idols for inspiration. K-pop keeps it fun with fashion, making many of the looks idols wear seem refreshing to fans. Styles for shoots and shows tend to be more dramatic, while airport and off-duty looks often embrace Korean street style. To find fashion "inspo," fans may look to concepts, promotions, or even airport stylings, and some fans buy items their favorite idols wear. Since idols commonly wear designer brands, companies geared toward Western K-pop fans create dupes that resemble looks idols have worn so that fans can emulate them.

IDOL AMBASSADORSHIPS & BRAND ENDORSEMENTS

Various beauty and fashion companies have capitalized on the popularity of K-pop by selecting idols to represent them as ambassadors or in promotional materials.

Idols appear in nearly every type of content you can think of, but magazines are extremely popular. Idols regularly appear on magazine covers, usually wearing pieces from big or up-and-coming fashion houses. They're styled in eye-catching ways to not only exhibit the idols' visuals but also showcase the clothes they're wearing.

Print and digital materials are often combined for the greatest impact. Fans like to collect magazines, so magazines often produce multiple collectible covers when an idol or group is featured. This promotes the idols while also giving partner brands exposure and guaranteed engagement from fans.

Idols also make in-person fashion appearances. When idols appear at events, they produce a high media impact. Many idols and fashion houses form long-term relationships for even more effect.

Idols have become ambassadors for brands around the world, including the most prestigious fashion houses. Ambassadors wear the fashion houses' clothes and take part in various campaign materials. Some notable ambassadors include G-Dragon for Chanel, YoonA for Miu Miu, Kai for Gucci, and Jimin for Tiffany & Co. These ambassadorships highlight the increasing demand for K-pop idols to participate in fashion.

In recent years, idols have become even more intertwined with fashion and are often invited to major fashion events. The Met Gala is one of fashion's biggest events, and several idols have been asked to attend over the years. In 2024, Stray Kids became the first to attend the Met Gala as an entire group.

Additionally, during fashion weeks, it's more common than ever to see K-pop idols take a break from their busy schedules to attend fashion shows. Some idols have even hit the runway, including NCT's Jeno, Stray Kid's Felix, BLACKPINK's Lisa, MONSTA X's Shownu, and IKON's DK.

CONCERNS RELATED TO FASHION & BEAUTY TRENDS

Appreciating Korean cultural can be exciting and enriching for K-pop fans. It encourages global interconnectedness and understanding through shared experiences. However, there are potential harms and concerns related to how Korean fashion and beauty trends are used.

The problem of cultural appropriation presents itself in two ways: fans may appropriate Korean culture, and idols may appropriate other cultures. Either can result in harm. K-pop concepts have, in some cases, reduced important aspects of certain cultures to mere aesthetics. Idols have appropriated other cultures by wearing blackface, using stereotypical images or gestures, making culturally insensitive comments, and engaging in similar types of discrimination. Likewise, certain groups of fans interact with K-pop on a shallow level without taking the time to truly understand Korean culture and how it differs from Western culture.

Another issue fans should consider is the hierarchical nature of Asian beauty and fashion. East Asians (i.e., Koreans, Japanese, and Chinese) tend to enjoy certain privileges unavailable to other Asians. This disparity is often related to colorism and the idea that the tone of a person's skin determines how they should be treated. Due to classicist and colonial influences, light skin is associated with the higher class and, thus, grants more chances for upward mobility.

These prejudices existed before K-pop, but the continued spread of colorist standards has encouraged potentially dangerous treatments like skin lightening. Such practices can cause a range of side effects, especially when performed under anesthesia. Side effects may include skin damage like rashes or facial swelling, kidney disorders, and mercury poisoning.

Korean beauty standards are strict, and idols are encouraged to fit the mold as closely as possible. Many fans want to emulate their idols, even if that means extreme practices like unhealthy diets, surgeries, and expensive products. Seeing idols as "perfect" may cause young fans especially to have low self-esteem.

In many cases, the idols' looks are strictly—and artificially—controlled. Idols may be told by their managers to avoid activities with heavy sun exposure to prevent tanning. Filters and other digital alterations are often used to maintain the look Korean beauty standards expect.

While there has been societal pushback against these strict standards, for now, fans should avoid idealizing these standards without considering the harmful downstream effects. There's nothing wrong with wanting to incorporate Korean style and beauty elements into fashion, but each fan must be careful to choose trends that coexist with a healthy overall lifestyle.

CHAPTER THREE:
K-POP MUSIC & PERFORMANCES

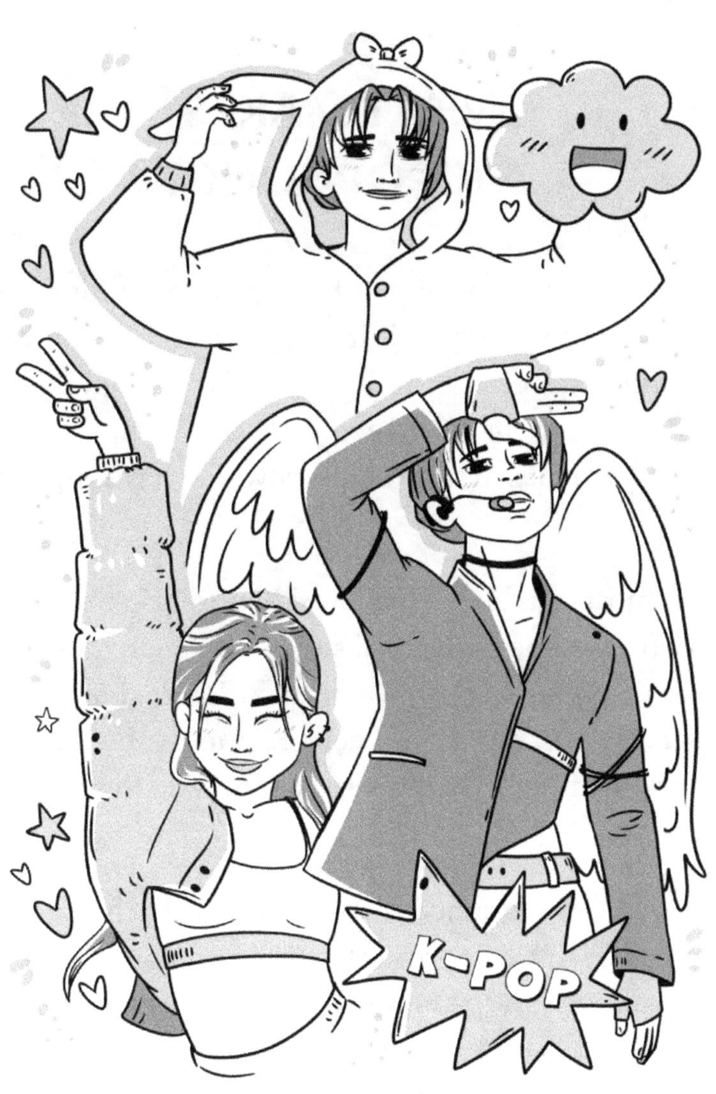

Even if you're not interested in anything else from this book, K-pop music and performances are sure to captivate you! From the making of songs to the influence of dance and performance, K-pop is made to capture the audience's attention with multi-sensory experiences that create lasting memories and inspire enthusiasm among fans.

WHAT MAKES
A K-POP SONG?

When you hear a K-pop song, it has a way of pulling you in and making you want to sing and dance, even if you don't know the words or choreography. Although there's no single definition of what makes K-pop its own genre, K-pop songs tend to have several key elements, which helps newbies have a good idea of what to expect.

One of the most notable elements of K-pop is genre blending. K-pop draws from some traditional styles of Korean music, but it also uses Western styles like hip-hop, jazz, R&B, dance, and Latin. Drawing from so many styles keeps K-pop fresh and allows each group and solo artist to define themselves with their own flavor of K-pop.

Structure is also important for K-pop songs. Each song is slightly different, but many have an intro, verse, chorus, second verse, chorus, break or bridge, and a final chorus. There may be additional choruses, riffs, or pre-choruses added as the songwriter sees fit. Rap can be included at various points, often during the bridge or between the chorus and verse.

If a group wants a K-pop song to be a hit, it's got to be well produced and catchy. Arrangements, sound engineering, and other sonic elements give K-pop a polished sound even when the lyrics aren't particularly complicated. K-pop songs often use simple, repetitive lyrics to appeal to listeners who don't speak Korean and add to the catchiness of the song. Writers craft hooks and melodies to ensure the entire song is structurally sound.

Additionally, K-pop lyrics often include different languages. Multilingual songs have become more popular as K-pop expanded around the world, but even in the early days, English group names and lyrics were used. Depending on a group's target audience, they may also use other languages such as Japanese, Mandarin, Thai, French, or Spanish.

Most songs will only use two languages at one time, but it's not unheard of to have three or more. For example, SF9's "O Sole Mio" includes six languages! Songs may also be translated into several different languages, and you commonly see Japanese or English versions of songs.

THE SIGNIFICANCE OF TITLE TRACKS

When introducing an artist's new era, title tracks are vital, as they give audiences an idea what to expect from the comeback. In Western music, a title track has the same name as the album it's on, but as you read in the previous list of definitions, the title track in K-pop is the song the group has chosen to represent their album.

While title tracks are often the first song a group releases after their previous comeback, they may also share pre-release tracks, which are B-sides used to help with promotions. The goal of pre-releases is to hype up the audience, then use the attention the pre-release earns to improve the success of the title track. Pre-releases have other benefits too, like adding listening numbers so that groups have a better chance of getting awards.

Mostly, title tracks are just one song, but in some cases, groups and solos include two or, on rare occasions, three. Double title tracks have been used by rookie and established groups alike, but it's often advantageous for new groups who want to prove themselves and debut strongly. BLACKPINK beat records, and in 2016 became the fastest debut song to get a PAK, when the group released the double tracks "WHISTLE" and "BOOMBAYAH." Other groups known for double track debuts include WINNER, ATEEZ, WENDY, ONE, and NCT U.

Having an iconic title track can define an artist's era, so each is carefully selected. Some groups have input in the title track, but companies usually make that decision. The success of a title track guarantees the album release will be a success—the start of a memorable comeback.

K-POP MUSIC VIDEOS

Music videos (MVs) are a big deal in K-pop because they help idols explore comeback concepts and reach global audiences. Viral K-pop MVs like "Gangnam Style" have shown that captivating videos can have a profound impact on an idol's success.

Most K-pop MVs are somewhere between three and five minutes long. Just like Western MVs, some include intros or conclusions to build a story, while others get right into the song. They usually include elaborate costumes, sets, and choreography to merge visual aesthetics with audio.

Companies bring in top professionals to create the best video from start to finish. This process usually begins with storyboarding, where a general design concept is created. This concept is drawn from the comeback's concept and elements of the song. Then the team moves into production design, which focuses on turning the storyboard into real elements, including set and styling. Once the visual elements are finalized, designers work to create lighting that sets the right mood and best features artists' faces.

The team must also think about cinematography, camera angles, and what shots to capture when the idols arrive. Special equipment and creativity are often required to fit all members in the frame and adhere to the concept. Sometimes, green screens or other tools are used to add special effects in post-production.

Once the foundation for a video is established, performance elements begin. Choreographers help idols learn and practice their dance moves, which can take weeks to master. The group usually has to perform the choreography multiple times so that the dance can be seen from different angles, sometimes in several locations. Of course, some shots feature storytelling moments or focus on certain members' parts rather than choreographed dances.

Even after recording has wrapped, there are still several steps to go before the MV is ready for release. Post-production involves a lot of effort to combine the recorded content into one streamlined project. Some elements take longer, especially when special effects are used. Post-production includes color-correction and audio adjustment as well. Editing magic can add a sense of movement and continuity that fans often don't notice, but they'll be able to tell if it's not there.

MVs are a huge investment in the K-pop world because companies know how important professional, eye-catching videos are. Popular videos can get hundreds of millions or even billions of views, and fans are always excited to see what aesthetics will be used.

K-POP DANCE & CHOREOGRAPHY

Dance is a staple of K-pop; without dance, the genre would lack its visual appeal and viral potential. Accordingly, idols focus extensively on dancing, and companies hire the best choreographers to bring songs to life and magic to performances.

From the start, dance has been a huge part of idol groups' images and performance. Over time, dancing skills have become increasingly important, and choreographies have become more elaborate. Dances must fit the song or concept perfectly. Otherwise, the success of a comeback will suffer. Idols train and practice for hours to perfect the moves and build the stamina they need to perform.

K-pop dances feature synchronized movement and elements from different styles like hip-hop and jazz. These dances tend to be high energy and may include tricks like flips, lifts, or other stunts. The style of dancing evolves as the songs do, making it impossible to know what choreography you may see next!

These days, idols commonly hold social media dance challenges that fans can then post online. Platforms like TikTok have embraced these dance challenges, and idols often collaborate with idols outside their group for cross-promotion potential.

Fans love to learn dances, and not just for social media. While K-pop dances can be difficult, fans can replicate many at home (though perhaps not as cleanly as idols), so K-pop dances are often part of their exercise routines.

THE ROLE OF
DANCE PRACTICES

Because dance is such a vital part of K-pop, it has become more than just a flourish for live performances and MVs. Choreography has become another way to connect fans with idols and promote new music. One way idols have maximized the role of dance is through dance practices.

Dance practices began as low-quality videos showcasing idols—especially groups—practicing their choreography. These videos gained popularity quickly because they showcase idols' dance skills and provide much-desired bonus content. These videos have evolved to be high quality but have retained a raw feel, as idols are usually in casual clothes inside a normal dance studio. In these videos, idols focus on dancing rather than singing so that fans can see their choreography and technique.

One feature that sets dance practices apart from MVs and live performances is the camera work and editing. Over the years, some camerawork has become more complex, but the goal is still to capture the dance rather than adding cuts. The editing is also less intense. Companies want to make practices look natural, so they leave out editing flourishes and visual effects to emphasize the choreography.

Dance videos have established themselves as an important part of K-pop. *Studio Choom,* a YouTube channel that curates a collection of one-take dance videos of prominent K-pop idols, opened in response to the trend. The channel uses lighting and several angles to highlight the dancing. While these videos are more upscale than traditional practice videos, they show the demand fans have for K-pop dance content.

Some viral dance practice videos include:

- BLACKPINK's "Kill This Love"
- IVE's "Love Dive"
- LE SSERAFIM's "FEARLESS"
- Stray Kids' "MANIAC"
- BTS's "Silver Spoon (Baepsae)"
- PSY ft. SUGA's "That That"
- (G)I-DLE's "My Bag"
- Red Velvet's "Feel My Rhythm"
- Jessi's "ZOOM"
- MOMOLAND's "BAAM"

K-POP FANDOMS
& FAN CHANTS

Fandoms are a major component of K-pop. Each group has its own fandom, a group of supporters who do whatever they can to help their favorite idols. Each fandom has its own name, such as BTS's Army and ATEEZ's ATINY. These names help fans identify each other, as well as other fandoms. Fandoms become close-knit groups (though divisions exist) and feel personally connected to the success of a solo or group. Without fandoms, K-pop wouldn't enjoy the level of success it does today.

Many fandoms have fanbases and pages, which organize fandom events and post updates about what's happening within the fandom. They're hubs for anyone looking to learn more about K-pop and participate in fandom activities. Fandoms have a huge presence on social media, but there are also in-person groups that gather to talk about their favorites and bond over their shared love of K-pop.

One example of what fandom does is organize fan chants. Fan chants are important for anyone attending a K-pop concert or event to show their support. Basically, these are brief cheers fans arrange to use during songs, and they help hype up idols and create a sense of camaraderie between fans.

Fandom is supposed to be a fun and enriching experience, but of course, friction within or between fandoms can get quite heated. Fans feel so connected to idols that some lash out and become protective of idols if they feel those idols are being disrespected. Fortunately, if you want to be part of a fandom, you can choose how to engage with other fans and preserve your own peace. However, you don't have to be formally involved in fandom to enjoy K-pop!

THE IMPORTANCE OF LIGHTSTICKS

Lightsticks are a special K-pop item that fans buy to support their group at live performances. Lightsticks are basically rods with a battery-powered light at the top, used at concerts the same way as phone flashlights (or, originally, lighters).

Each group has its own unique light stick that's designed to reflect the vibes of the group. Their shape and size can vary greatly, but most lightsticks feature the group's logo. Cherry Bullet's light stick shows how creative designers can get; it's shaped like a colorful red gun, which diverges from the usual wand shape. The names of the sticks are fun too, such as SHINee's *shabat,* so named because fans joked that it was so bright it could be used an emergency light.

Performances are enhanced by lightsticks, illuminating the audience with vibrant colors to generate dazzling effects. They create what fans call an "ocean," a sea of moving lights looking on at their idols on the stage. Lightsticks unite fans and add a visual element to the show to highlight the performers.

Not only does the glow from the lightsticks look cool, but it also helps cheer on the idols and show their fans' support. A black ocean, in which fans aren't using or have turned off their light sticks, is a sign of disinterest or even displeasure. Fans have used black oceans to protest or show disapproval with an idol or group.

Black oceans may also be used by rival fans as part of fan wars. Thus, the way fans use—or don't use—their lightsticks has surprisingly profound meanings in K-pop.

K-POP COMEBACKS: WHAT TO EXPECT

K-pop releases are formal and structured, which distinguishes them from Western releases. Comebacks are a big deal in K-pop because they establish a new era in an idol's career. Obviously, comebacks are prime time for new content, so fans get extra excited when a new comeback is upon them.

A comeback occurs when artists return with new music, generally a new album. Sometimes, this is an LP, but for others, they'll release a full-length EP. Comebacks may take place after just a few months but can be over a year from their last release. It all depends on the artist, along with their company and management team.

The leadup to the release of an album is vital to any comeback. Fans prepare projects to stream and purchase albums with the goal of creating the largest possible number of sales in the first week. This momentum helps get the best chart positions for the album, and fanbases lead the charge to organize efforts.

While the focus of any comeback is the music, it also includes performances on music shows. The first live performance of a comeback is a comeback stage that introduces the music, choreography, and overall artistic vision. Usually, only a title track—and potentially one other track—will be performed on music shows, and the bulk of the attention is on the title track.

During this time, fans can help with efforts to win music shows and earn artists the chance for awards through streaming, voting, and album purchases.

Artists have a lot of promotional opportunities during comebacks such as going on variety shows, radio shows, and YouTube channels. They also tend to post additional content on their YouTube channel and social media, trying to get as much exposure as possible during the first few weeks of a comeback.

Artists also engage with fans in several ways during comebacks, including fan meets, signing events, and special performances. Often, comebacks lead to a tour associated with the album.

LIVE STAGES & MUSIC SHOWS

Live stages and music shows are some of the most exciting parts of a K-pop comeback, offering a large stream of content to keep fans constantly entertained. While Western fans likely already understand basic concept of a music show, they have a different culture in South Korea as an integral part of any idol's comeback.

In South Korea, several music shows seek to determine and present the most popular songs each week. Every show has its own criteria for winning, but they usually include factors like pre-voting, live voting, album sales, MV streams, and social media.

These shows play an integral role in comeback promotions, giving idols the chance to attract new fans and bolster their success by winning. When idols win across all major broadcasters with one track, they get an all-kill.

Music shows usually feature both pre-recordings and live broadcasts, attended by fans. Pre-recordings are typically open to verified fan club members because fan clubs run entry into the pre-recordings. Fans who attend pre-recordings usually get perks like small gifts or exclusive photocards. During pre-recordings, artists go through several takes, and live broadcasts during the show include some of the pre-recording winners.

The sheer number of shows and ranking criteria can be confusing at first, but for now, all you need to know about are the main shows and why they're important.

Inkigayo

Inkigayo is run by SBS and airs on Sundays. It's famously hard to get into because of limited studio space. *Inkigayo* is also known for backstage pictures, and many idols take pictures by the stairs. If you see a picture of an idol or group by a stairway with a red rail, it's probably the *Inkigayo* stairs.

M Countdown

M Countdown is run by Mnet and airs every Thursday. It's noted for popular performance videos with impressive camerawork and is responsible for the popularity of face and relay dance cams. International fans also like *M Countdown* because it gives them more opportunities to participate in voting.

Music Bank

Music Bank is a KBS show that airs every Friday. Besides the music, *Music Bank* is known for its fun backstage content. The show also does special stages, which break up the expected stages with fun surprises. Like *Inkigayo*, idols often pose by *Music Bank*'s stairs, sometimes inside a round section of the silver rail.

Show Champion

MBC Plus broadcasts *Show Champion* on Wednesdays. This show was an early adopter of the Triple Crown system, which prohibits artists from winning with the same song for more than three consecutive weeks.

Show! Music Core

MBC broadcasts *Show! Music Core* each Saturday with a focus on quality singing. In 2014, the show even prohibited lip syncing! *Show! Music Core* is also popular for hosting fan meet events before and after the show.

The Show

The Show is broadcast on SBS M on Tuesdays, and it tends to be the go-to show for new or up-and-coming artists. The intimate environment of *The Show* makes attending a special experience for audiences.

Simply K-Pop

Simply K-pop is aired by Arirang TV every Friday. Although it's a lesser-known show because it's broadcast on the English network, this actually makes it more accessible for many global audiences.

Music Universe K-909

JTBC's *Music Universe K-909* is another Saturday show. It may not be as widely known to international audiences, but it stands out for its in-depth interviews with idols and focus on quality content.

CONCERTS & FAN MEETS

If you're looking to see an idol in person, concerts and fan meets are great opportunities to experience an in-person (if distant) connection to idols. They'll make you feel more involved with the K-pop community. After all, there's nothing quite like spending time with an idol in the same room!

What to Expect from K-Pop Concerts

While you may have been to a concert before, the typical Western concern isn't quite the same as a K-pop one. K-pop concerts have certain norms and traditions that fans should know before they attend. Once you know what to expect, you'll be ready to truly appreciate the high energy and camaraderie of a K-pop concert.

The first thing you need to know about a K-pop concert is that you'll need to be ready to take it in with all your senses. Music, dancing, and visuals are carefully arranged to capture the intended tone of the concert and make sure the audience is constantly entertained. That's not so different from any other concert, but in K-pop, the fans are part of the overall effect, using light sticks and fan chants to become active parts of the show.

You may also notice that people dress up in fun outfits when attending K-pop concerts. They may take inspiration from the groups they're seeing or just wear something generally fashionable. While it's good to dress up a little and showcase your style, remember to wear something comfortable that you can move around in, and take extra care to wear comfortable shoes. Finding a blend between fashionable and comfortable magnifies the concert experience, and you'll never look out of place.

Some fans also opt to wear ear protection during the concert. K-pop concerts can get pretty rowdy, and fans often cheer quite loudly, so earplugs are probably a good idea. Specially designed earplugs allow you to hear the music while protecting your ears from the noise around you. Preserve your hearing so that you can have many more years of concerts to come.

When purchasing tickets, you may notice that groups offer hi-touch sessions after the show, which provide fans with brief moments of interaction with idols. Sometimes hi-touch is free, but hi-touch is generally a VIP upgrade.

Finally, don't be afraid to socialize! It can be nice to chat with other fans around you or simply be in the same area as others who share your interest in K-pop. Of course, always prioritize safety and make sure you aren't giving away personal information, but most fans are good natured and love meeting others who share their passion.

Connecting Through Fan Meets

Fan meets are an interactive way for idols to engage their audiences and connect with fans. They usually involve a performance as well as games and interviews. Some fan meets involve additional elements such as hi-touch events and photo ops. Generally, fan meets are relatively relaxed with a smaller crowd than a concert.

In-person fan meets mostly take place in Korea, but in recent years, virtual events have become more common. While these events can feel somewhat distant and detached, they're a good option for overseas fans without the means or desire to travel to Korea for an in-person fan meet.

Of course, fan meets require a ticket, and they usually sell out quickly. International fans often have a hard time getting in-person tickets, but you can still try for them or look for online events. Fan meets typically have both a general sale and a presale, though the presale is often reserved for members of official fan clubs. In some cases, different package options are available, so make plans before ticketing day.

CHAPTER FOUR: K-POP IDOLS & THEIR JOURNEY

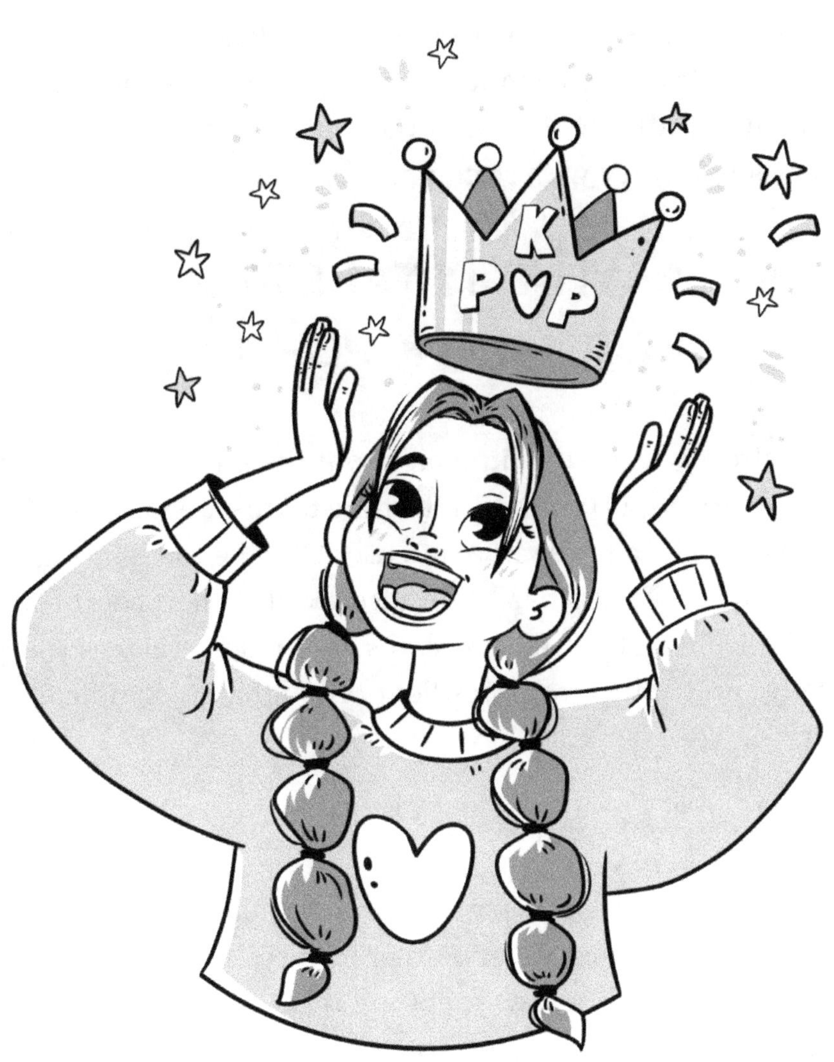

K-pop idols must endure a long journey if they want to have a lasting career. Unfortunately, the success of many groups is fleeting, and some idols can do everything right and never attain the success they crave.

Thus, while there are tons of success stories in K-pop, there are even more stories of heartbreak and disappointment. From starting as a trainee to venturing into a solo career, K-pop artists have many hurdles to leap, and they must learn to navigate each step of their journey with strength.

WHAT IT TAKES TO BECOME A K-POP IDOL

You've already learned a little bit about the importance and rigor of training for K-pop idols, but it's time to dive deeper into the life of a K-pop trainee to see how intense it can be for aspiring idols. Trainees not only work hard; they also sacrifice their youth, hoping for a chance to follow their dreams. To debut, trainees must be mentally and physically resilient enough to complete their training.

What Trainees Learn

Each company has its own specific training process, but all companies share an expectation that trainees will commit fully to their training, which means spending most of their waking hours going to classes and pushing their bodies to their limits. Many trainees train for years before making a debut, but even quick studies require weeks or months of training.

At the heart of the lessons, trainees learn dance, vocals, and rap, as these skills are the main components of K-pop. However, trainees also study other subjects to prepare for the challenges they'll endure as idols, including language classes. Obviously, foreign trainees must learn Korean, but it's also common to learn languages such as Japanese, English, or Mandarin. Companies teach these in hopes that language skills will help soloists or groups break into global markets and make trainees more versatile.

Other topics include media training, health and fitness, personal image development, and team building. To be an idol, a trainee must possess a wide range of skills and prove they can adapt to various situations they may encounter.

Tracking Trainees' Progress

K-pop companies track their idols' progress with evaluations, generally held monthly. At JYP, one form of a monthly evaluation was a "free monthly test," a mini showcase performed in front of staff, family, and friends. Trainees organized choreographies, sang live without backing vocals, and had to do freestyle dance one at a time.

While this is just one example, generally, evaluations are designed to push trainees out of their comfort zone and simulate challenges they may face as idols. These evaluations help companies track the progress of idols, but they also help idols work better as individuals and teams.

The Dangers Trainees Face

Although trainees take part in an exciting and fulfilling development process, their lives are far from glamorous; many companies perpetuate harmful expectations and create conditions that risk the mental and physical health of their talent.

Being a trainee is risky as well because there's no guarantee that an individual will ever debut. Trainees can work for years and end up scrambling to figure out what to do next. It can be hard for failed trainees to move forward with their lives, and they often feel they must start over to find a new path.

Even if a trainee makes it into a group or becomes a soloist, not all idols are successful, and many struggle to stay afloat after debut. Groups may quickly disband after debuting or soloists' careers may fizzle out despite all their efforts. Thus, what seems like an exciting career opportunity can quickly shatter.

The Korean training system is a lot like a factory. The process is regimented and encourages idol to conform. Companies focus on profit, sometimes at the expense of vulnerable youths who are desperate to make their dreams come true at any cost. Companies have strict rules. They often forbid trainees from dating, separate male and female trainees, ban social media use, and monitor cell phones.

Trainees get up early in the morning and stay up until late at night. Many don't get enough sleep, and with all the physical exertion they put themselves through, injuries and fatigue can add to the already huge challenges they face.

Idols are expected to look a certain way, and as a result, diet and body image concerns can become harmful. Trainees and idols are expected to maintain their looks and as many Korean beauty standards as possible. Companies sometimes put trainees on dangerous diets to reach these standards.

Momo from TWICE was once told to lose 15 pounds in one week before she debuted. She ate nothing but ice cubes and reported being so scared for her health that she was afraid she'd go to sleep and not wake up. This diet was not healthy or sustainable, and it shows the pressure and harm that trainees can come under.

There's also the matter of finances. Companies invest money into training, education, and other required expenses, but trainees often have to pay for additional expenses. Although trainees may receive small monetary awards for certain things like being on a survival show, most aren't paid until they've debuted. Because of this, accruing debt during training is common, especially for trainees in small companies who may be expected to pay the company back for their training. Some companies cancel debt if a trainee eventually debuts.

THE DEBUT PROCESS

Making the transition from trainee to idol is a big step even after the extensive training that trainees go through. Companies must determine who should join which group, and once they've formed a group, they must establish the group's sound, tone, and interpersonal dynamics. Companies are very careful with the debut process—after all, a group can only debut once, and if they don't start strong, they may not get a comeback.

Trainees are put into debut projects based on evaluations. While talent is important, the projects will often have a certain direction the company wants the group to go. Groups will evolve after forming, but companies like to know the debut project has a foundation before choosing members. The lineup for a group isn't permanent at this stage. Companies may still make changes and even cut members if they don't "fit" properly.

Once a pre-debut group is formed, they start training together. This process helps form group dynamics and gives the company an idea of what tweaks to make before debut. At this point, the members of the group receive even more training, such as learning to interact with the media. The company will also showcase the group more to introduce them to the public. Many K-pop fans pay close attention to pre-debut groups to learn about the idols before they become popular. Companies like to build a fanbase that will support the group's release right away, adding security to a project.

Throughout the debut process, the artists' teams work on crafting the perfect track. They must also design a debut concept, promotional strategies, member roles, choreography, and visuals. Finalizing these details involves tons of preparation, but they're what makes a debut successful. Finally, idols start practicing and recording their first release and prepare promotional materials.

With fundamentals in place, the group is ready to debut. They get to release their music, go on music shows, and start promoting the project they've worked so hard on. If all goes well, they'll have the chance to make a comeback and go through the content-creation process all over again.

THE ROLE OF ENTERTAINMENT COMPANIES

The main creators of K-pop groups are entertainment companies. While rare cases of independent music creators, such as Dream Perfect Regime (DPR), do pop up, most popular K-pop acts are backed by a company. The Big Three—SM, YG, and JYP—have dominated K-pop since the genre's early years.

Of course, with the success of BTS, HYBE has also made a name for itself. These companies shape and manage idols' careers, so knowing a bit about them will help you understand just how much influence they have.

SM Entertainment

The first K-pop company to be created was SM Entertainment, which quickly established itself as a pioneer, gaining its first taste of success with H.O.T. SM was created by Lee Soo-Man in 1995, who wanted to innovate Korean music and create a strong foundation for the future of K-pop, which was still in its infancy.

The company is known for its huge roster of successful groups and soloists. Some standout artists from SM's history include:

- H.O.T.
- Girls' Generation
- Red Velvet
- TVXQ
- aespa
- SHINee

- BoA
- EXO
- S.E.S.
- f(x)
- NCT
- Super Junior
- RIIZE
- SuperM (collaboration group)

YG Entertainment

Yang Hyun Suk, a member of Seo Taiji and Boys, established YG Entertainment shortly after SM Entertainment in 1996. YG Entertainment's goal was to make music with distinct style. YG didn't just want to make a lot of music; the company wanted to guarantee their music was unique and stylistically strong. This drive for musical diversity and unique talent established YG as one of the top entertainment companies in Korea.

Famous artists that have been signed under YG Entertainment include:

- BLACKPINK
- 1TYM
- BIGBANG
- Jeon Somi
- CL
- iKON
- WINNER
- Tablo
- 2NE1

- T.O.P.
- Treasure
- BABYMONSTER
- G-Dragon

JYP Entertainment

In 1997, Park Jin Young created JYP Entertainment, which pushed K-pop even further by reaching for success in global markets. Although JYP did well early on with solo artists and G.O.D., the company eventually achieved success overseas with groups like the Wonder Girls. Today, groups like TWICE and Stray Kids continue to show JYP's dreams of global success.

Some key groups JYP Entertainment has signed include:

- Stray Kids
- TWICE
- GOT7
- ITZY
- DAY6
- MiSaMo
- 2PM
- Wonder Girls
- Rain
- Jeon Somi
- MISS A
- NMIXX

HYBE

In 2005, Bang Shi Hyuk established Big Hit Entertainment, which eventually became HYBE. The company started small and initially struggled to compete with the Big Three; however, with the debut of BTS, HYBE became a standout in entertainment and showed the fullest potential of K-pop as a global genre.

The company has continued to create artists, hoping to build on BTS's success. While HYBE has enjoyed a great deal of success, the company faces challenges in asserting itself as a long-term K-pop power. HYBE has had many issues recently, including evidence of possible *sajaegi,* the illegal practice of manipulating charts. Insults and attacks targeted at other groups have caused further public outrage.

Prominent groups of HYBE include:

- BTS
- TXT
- NU'EST (via Pledis Entertainment purchase)
- SEVENTEEN (via Pledis Entertainment purchase)

Other Companies

While the Big Three and HYBE have dominated K-pop in recent years, other companies have also created successful groups. HYBE's success has encouraged other companies to dream big and bring the best out of their idol groups. For instance, in 2023, MAMAMOO became the first girl group outside the Big Three to get more than two billion streams on *Melon,* a popular streaming platform in Korea.

Additionally, many members of groups have signed on as soloists with smaller companies. There's certainly room for these companies to grow and create a space for themselves in K-pop, especially with the help of international audiences.

Some examples of other companies and their artists include:

- Cube Entertainment: (G)I-DLE and BTOB
- Polaris Entertainment: LOONA and Tripleme
- KQ Entertainment (Under Seven Seasons): ATEEZ
- Starship Entertainment: BOYFRIEND, SISTAR, MONSTA X, CRAVITY
- FNC Entertainment: AOA and SF9
- Kakao M: IU, The Boyz, Apink
- Fantagio Entertainment: ASTRO and Weki Meki

THE PRESSURE OF
BEING AN IDOL

An idol's work never stops, no matter how well established they are. To stay at the top of their game, idols must constantly push themselves, enduring both physical and mental challenges.

Many idols struggle to balance their work with their personal lives. They spend long days training or promoting, so by the time they get home, it's time for bed. Idols frequently don't get enough sleep before they must get up and go back to work.

Due to all the stress they put their bodies under, it's not unheard of for idols to work so hard that they pass out from exhaustion. f(x)'s Krystal fainted on multiple occasions during her time in the group. In 2010, she fainted during a performance because she'd only been sleeping a few hours a day. Hyeri from Girl's Day collapsed after finishing a performance and had to be carried off the stage, unable to stand on her own. These are merely two of many artists who've fainted due to the stress of idol life.

Several idols have also had major onstage accidents. In 2009, SHINee performed at Music Bank, and Onew lost consciousness after nearly being hit by a large piece of lighting equipment. Red Velvet's Wendy was seriously injured while the group was rehearsing for the musical festival SBS Gayo Daejeon. The accident, caused by improper stage marking, resulted in Wendy falling six and a half feet. She fractured her wrist, pelvis, and parts of her face, requiring extensive recovery time.

For all the joy K-pop brings, there's been a lot of heartache as well. High-profile suicides of K-pop stars like ASTRO's Moonbin, SHINee's Kim Jonghyun, KARA's Goo Hara, and Sulli all show a darker side of K-pop. The constant pressure K-pop stars face can lead to mental health struggles, especially in an industry that often breeds mental health issues without doing enough to help idols navigate their struggles.

Depression, anxiety, cyberbullying, harassment, and public scrutiny can make it hard for idols to keep their heads above water. Add in rigorous schedules and idol-specific stress, and the result is a recipe for tragedy. However, while mental health is still somewhat of a taboo topic in Korea, it's becoming more common for idols to care for their mental health along with their physical bodies.

Idols are supposed to set a good moral example at all times. Anything less than the best behavior can receive huge public backlash, even if it's something relatively minor or unintentional. Sometimes, even dating—like any normal person—might cause public outrage.

IDOL FAN SERVICE: WHAT IT IS & WHY IT MATTERS

One way idols interact with their fans is through fan service. The term *fan service* likely originated from its often less-savory usage in Japanese anime and manga, but it has since become an important part of idol fandom culture. In K-pop, fan service refers to anything idols do specifically to appeal to the fans' desires or fantasies. This behavior has become a major part of idols' jobs, so companies learn what fans want in order to teach idols what methods to use.

Through fan service, idols build their reputations and create an image for themselves. Idols use fan service to make fans feel closer, and they end up with more dedicated fans who will support them with each new comeback.

Fan service can be relatively simple, such as having fancams and facecams to focus on each member so that fans can watch their biases. These cams allow fans a glimpse into their biases' habits and eccentricities, which make them interesting to watch. Other forms of fan service include idols dressing in certain outfits or using *aegyo*. Male idols may do things like show off their abs or other muscles.

One of the best forms of fan service is taking time to make fans feel personally connected. Live streams and messaging platforms help fans feel valued, and the more genuine the interaction seems, the stronger their connection with the idol or group becomes. Hugs, eye contact, and playfulness are all methods idols use to build a deeper bond with fans.

Fan service isn't just about the relationship between fans and their idols, though; it's also about the dynamics between idols. For groups, fan service between members is crucial. Fans like to see idols getting along with other members of their group and having fun together. Members may act affectionately toward one another through skinship or inside jokes.

When idols use fan service, they create a more interactive experience for fans, making them more invested in the idols themselves rather than just the music. Fan service creates excitement and adds an additional layer to the K-pop experience. Some idols use it more than others, but all idols must use it to some extent.

K-POP REALITY SHOWS & DOCUMENTARIES

Reality shows and documentaries have emerged as a growing form of K-pop engagement. While survival shows have been around for a while, they've become especially popular in the past several years because of shows such as *Produce 101*, *I-Land*, and *Sixteen*. Reality shows and documentaries help expand awareness of K-pop and give fans behind-the-scenes content.

On survival shows, contestants compete to debut in a group or solo project a company (or, sometimes, multiple companies) are trying to create. Viewers get a peek at the process trainees go through and all the highs and lows involved. These shows are designed to be intense and full of pressure to create suspense for the viewers. They also commonly include fan voting, which may be combined with scores given by the company. *Produce 101*, for example, empowers viewers by opting not to have a judging panel.

These shows make a lot of sense for companies because they create huge fanbases for groups on the show, making fans feel more invested because they played an active part in the group's creation and eventual debut. Survival shows also help the audience get to know members by watching them overcome challenging experiences. Fans root harder than ever for their favorites to succeed.

Some groups that came from survival shows include:

- Wanna One
- IZ*ONE
- MONSTA X
- Stray Kids
- ENHYPEN
- TREASURE
- I'LLIT
- TWICE
- KATSEYE
- Kep1er
- P NATION
- ZEROBASEONE
- MOMOLAND

While survival shows are usually geared more toward Korean audiences and existing K-pop fans, documentaries are more popular internationally. Groups may make documentaries to show behind-the-scenes content and explore their development. Other documentaries focus on exploring what K-pop is as a genre and how it works.

Several documentaries have been created to get the attention of Western audiences. For example, the documentary *K-Pop Idols*, released by Apple TV+, featured the global group Blackswan, Korean American artist Jessi, and the more traditional group CRAVITY. The documentary shows what K-pop stars go through and discusses the globalization of K-pop.

INTERNATIONAL IDOLS IN K-POP

With the increasing attention K-pop is attracting around the globe, it makes sense that K-pop groups have become more international. There are dozens of foreign K-pop idols in the industry today, and various companies have put more emphasis on creating international K-pop groups.

Some notable examples of idols who were born or raised in foreign countries include:

- Stray Kids' Bang Chan and Felix are Australian.
- BLACKPINK's Lisa is from Thailand.
- BLACKPINK's Rosé was born in New Zealand and raised in Australia.
- IVE's Rei is Japanese.

- TWICE's Mina, Momo, and Sana are Japanese.
- TWICE's Tzuyu was born in Taiwan.
- SEVENTEEN's Joshua was born in the United States.
- SEVENTEEN's Jun and The8 were born in China.
- LE SSERAFIM's Kazhua is Japanese.
- NMIXX's Lily is Australian.
- TEMPEST's Hanbin is Vietnamese.
- Blackswan's Fatou was born in Senegal.

What Foreign Idols Offer

Including foreign idols is a good way to appeal to international audiences. They speak foreign languages and draw fans who might not otherwise feel connected to K-pop. Many foreign idols—especially those from Western countries—do have Korean heritage, making them appealing to both fans from their home country and Korean audiences. As K-pop becomes more global, it's natural for idols to do so as well.

International K-Pop Groups

For a long time, K-pop companies have reached for international success. While this was originally through existing K-pop groups, in the past several years, companies have designed groups with the specific intention of focusing on global markets. Some of these groups don't even include Korean members, and many are made in conjunction with Western labels.

There have been several attempts to create an international K-pop group. In 2019, SM created a collaborative group called SuperM. SuperM took members from several popular SM groups to create the "Avengers of K-pop." Although this group was Korean, the goal was to take the top talent and form a group specifically for international consumption.

Unfortunately, the group did not achieve the desired levels of success; the pandemic, members' military service, and controversies around one member named Lucas left the new group without much momentum. However, the vision of an international K-pop group didn't die with SuperM.

JYP Entertainment joined forces with U.S.-based Republic Records to form VCHA, envisioned as a global girl group under the K-pop system. The competition show *A2K* brought together six girls with a range of ethnicities and backgrounds, and the group debuted in early 2024 with "Girls of the Year."

Although the group's debut was met with anticipation, fans became worried when member Kaylee went on an indefinite hiatus due to health issues. A few months later, the group canceled several performances and became inactive other than sporadic posts. VHCA's early stumbles show both the potential and struggles that international K-pop groups face.

Shortly after JYP launched its global group project, other companies developed their own international groups. HYBE and Geffen Records created a survival show, *The Debut: The Dream Academy*, to select the six members that would become KATSEYE. A documentary called *Pop Star Academy: KATSEYE* was released on Netflix in August 2024 to show the behind-the-scenes process of training the finalists and their journey on the survival show.

KATSEYE includes members of various ethnicities and races from the United States, Switzerland, the Philippines, and Korea. The exposure KATSEYE received from the Netflix show helped the group gain momentum and attention from international audiences.

SOLO CAREERS IN K-POP

It has become increasingly common for idols to use their groups' success as a launching pad for a solo career. It's usually easier for artists to find success as a group, but in recent years, soloists have gained traction, especially those from big groups.

Members of groups like BTS and BLACKPINK have released solo projects to amazing success. Recent hits like Jungkook's "Seven" and Rosé's "APT" have shown not only the popularity soloists have in Korea but also the great potential to capture global audiences. Group members can excel as soloists, allowing fans to see new sides of their favorite idols.

There are several reasons why a group member may choose to go solo. One of the major ones is that, when a group disbands or becomes inactive, members usually still want to partake in K-pop. Some might choose other careers, such as hosting or acting, but many at least want to try solo work.

Even active members of a group may also want to work on solo projects. SHINee is an example of a group that still has comebacks while allowing each member to also work on solo projects. Solo projects are a great way for artists to express more of their personal stories and artistry, and it's beneficial to have an existing fanbase in place to help idols launch their solo careers.

Another major reason idols try solo work is military service. In South Korea, all men between the ages of 18 and 35 are required to serve in the military for 18 to 24 months, depending on the type of service. While there are some cases of exemption, most male idols are required to serve.

Generally, men choose to perform military service in their early 20s, but idols can usually defer their service until they're 28 to avoid interruptions while they establish their careers. In some groups, members go around the same time, but often, the members stagger their enlistment. While in the miliary, members cannot engage in professional activities, so other members may use that time to work on solo projects.

Soloists must be careful when releasing music, showing respect for the group they come from while also demonstrating their unique personalities. This process requires carefully crafting their solo debut and working with teams to bring their project to life. They may dip their toes into solo work with original soundtracks, which help them display their solo potential before they dive all the way in.

No matter what strategy artists choose to take, they must ensure their fans feel as though they're going on a new journey together. Solo work should feel like a bonus rather than a replacement for a group's work.

CHAPTER FIVE:
K-POP CULTURE & COMMUNITY

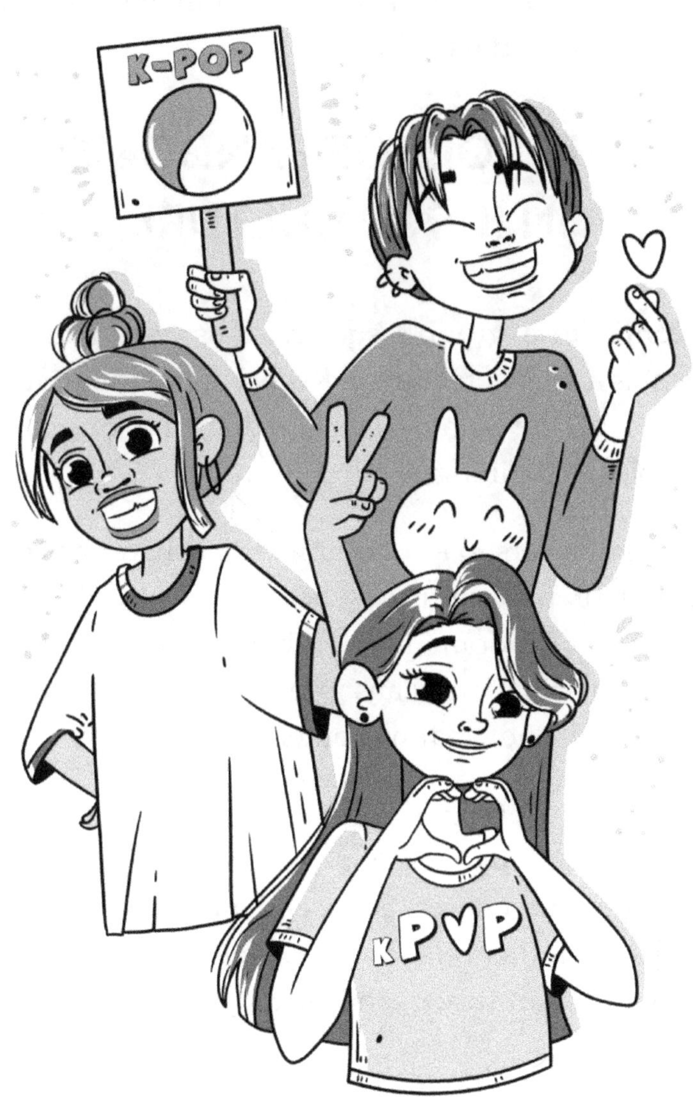

By now, you've probably realized that K-pop is about much more than the music. While the music itself can be satisfying, most K-pop fans also appreciate the culture and community that come with being a K-pop fan. These are the parts of K-pop that bring people from different backgrounds together and show the power of fandom, fan expression, and the continued growing global demand for K-pop and its culture.

THE ROLE OF FANDOMS IN K-POP CULTURE

When it comes to a group's success, fans are vital. Active fan involvement is a crucial feature of K-pop, and without it, the genre just wouldn't be the same. Thus, fandom has one of the most important roles in defining K-pop culture.

The term *fandom* refers to a community that shares an interest in a certain aspect of pop culture, whether it's music, TV, movies, books, or sports. Fandoms involve both passive enjoyment and community participation. Fans are actively engaged through voting, streaming, and creating content.

One major benefit to fandom is that it has a low barrier of entry while also building huge levels of support that an artist can rely on. Without fandom, interest is dependent on whether a song hits with the general audience. However, fandoms can create enough buzz that mainstream success follows.

The fun of fandom is that members can connect with others who have similar interests and biases. People from different backgrounds can work on shared projects, creating a social

92

connection and a sense of being a crucial part of that group's success. Fandom, therefore, creates an investment, making fans more likely to continue showing support even when an artist goes through a rough patch.

In K-pop fandoms, fanbases or popular fan accounts usually lead fandom efforts, but everyone is welcome to join in and do what they can to promote their group. More experienced fans help new fans understand the rules and parameters for efforts like voting, buying, and streaming. The goal is to pool collective resources to maximize results, whereas acting independently, fans would likely waste resources or miss opportunities.

Social media is a key fandom hub, but for less popular groups, you may have to look through several platforms to see which have the most active fans. Checking out K-pop forums and simple web searches can also help you get started if you want to join fandom activities. When you start connecting with other fans, you'll be introduced to that group's fan efforts in no time.

In response to the dominant role of fandom, companies, and their artists create content designed to encourage and cater to fandom. For example, different album versions encourage fans to purchase content for a chance to obtain certain photocards or other collectibles. Even digital albums may have alternate covers or versions with added voice memos from members, leading fans to buy more copies and even create fundraising drives to make purchases.

This connection between company and fandom is essential for K-pop, so fans have a huge influence; if a company is mistreating an idol, for instance, fans can use their influence to advocate for idols.

They may take actions such as sending a protest truck with an LED sign to deliver a message. In extreme scenarios, fans may even boycott content until the company changes its tune. Large fandoms often help define the continued path of an artist and, when needed, serve as artists' protectors.

The life of a K-pop fan is anything but dull, and fandoms can become forces to be reckoned with. When fandoms are attacked, whether by other fandoms or outsiders, they band together to resist. Fan wars are generally stressful and unwanted, but fandoms sometimes find themselves having to report or resist harmful behavior from members of another group. In these cases, the goal should be to limit engagement, reducing tension without letting harmful statements stand.

Healthy fandom activities include connections with other fandoms. While fan wars can break out when fans are competing to bring their idols to success, inter-fandom collaborations can be especially powerful when used strategically. Two or more fandoms can team up to achieve shared goals and take mutually beneficial action.

For instance, if a vote allows participants to choose both a boy group and a girl group, a fandom from each category can team up to add votes for both groups. Collaboration between fandoms may also take place when two artists collaborate on music or other endeavors.

THE IMPORTANCE OF
STREAMING & VOTING

Two important forms of fandom participation are streaming and voting. These are among the most common activities across all K-pop fandoms. Streaming and voting help groups become more successful, which shows companies that they're worth future investment. Without these two activities, groups or soloists can struggle to grow and may ultimately disband.

Streaming

No matter which musical fandom you're part of, streaming is likely part of the equation. Streaming platforms not only earn artists sales numbers, but they also increase a song's reach, which then builds an even bigger audience for artists. K-pop fans take streaming numbers very seriously and never want to be beaten by their competition. They're especially diligent about streaming during a comeback, but dedicated fans stream as much as possible to maintain numbers and reach streaming milestones faster.

Each platform has its own rules, but generally, you should avoid repeating songs or albums without other filler content. Streaming platforms filter out streams that seem like spam, so fans have to plan their streaming playlists carefully. Usually, adding a few songs between a single or album will do the trick, so don't stress too much when you first get started with streaming.

That may all sound complicated, but it doesn't have to be! One way K-pop fans have maximized their streaming is through *Stationhead* and other platforms that allow fans to stream songs at the same time, sort of like listening to the radio. These platforms use a subscription to streaming services to allow hosts to play songs. This makes streaming easy because the hosts play music for everybody, making sure to add in filler songs so that plays won't be filtered. Other fans also create and share streaming playlists, which you can use when you stream.

When in doubt, pay attention to what other fans are doing. Each comeback, fans usually create content with the "dos and don'ts" of streaming to keep everyone aware in case platforms have updated their filtering behaviors. At the end of the day, you want to stream well to support your favorites, but if you make mistakes, it isn't the end of the world. The goal should always be to have fun and try your best. If it ever stops being fun, that's a good sign that you should take a step back.

Voting

Voting allows fans to support their artists in a range of settings, including music shows, award shows, and fandom competitions. Fans like to prove their dedication and the superiority of their bias by getting as many wins as possible, even in relatively minor competitions.

One key area of voting is for music shows. Just as most Korean music shows include streaming in their criteria, it's common to include voting as well. Each show has a different weight for voting and how it impacts the final results. For example, *Show Champion* has a significant pre-vote, which accounts for 40 percent of the ranking. Meanwhile, *Music Bank* doesn't have a direct fan vote, only a viewer panel survey that includes randomly chosen registered viewers of the KBS survey panel. Some shows only have a pre-vote, while other shows have two categories: live vote and pre-vote.

Fans also vote for certain awards, including Korean and international awards. You'll learn more about award shows soon, but for some, voting may either decide or contribute to the win. Some awards aren't fan voted, so staying aware of those that are is one of the main tasks of fanbases. Votes may be one time per competition, but they're often daily, so some fans use multiple accounts to vote more than once. However, some competitions limit how much you can vote from one device. It can get pretty complicated, which is why fanbases often share information when a vote is ongoing.

Fan voting is also a key part of survival shows; often, the lineup of a group will be determined, at least in part, by a fan vote. Consequently, if you want an idol to debut with a group on a survival show, make sure you vote! Voting rules vary from show to show, but many are open to international voters.

Sometimes, various platforms hold special votes targeting certain idols based on things like dancing, original soundtracks, and visuals, many of which reward the winner. For example, fans may buy points to vote for birthday rewards; the prize is often an ad campaign supporting an idol or similar promotional measures.

You may also vote on social media polls. In exchange for engagement, the pages add extra votes to a specified voting campaign. For instance, they may offer five votes for whoever wins the poll and seven votes for whoever shows proof of engagement (usually via a series of tasks requiring additional effort and engagement with the host). Thus, fans can bolster their votes by engaging with outside parties.

Voting can be complex, so don't worry if you still have questions. Most will be answered when you get involved and start engaging with other fans.

VOTING & STREAMING FOR MUSIC SHOWS

The book has already described the main music shows and what they're all about, but now it's time to take that knowledge a step further and learn each voting show's criteria. Pay close attention if you want to partake in music show voting and streaming.

Inkigayo

On *Inkigayo*, songs from the top 150 of the Circle Digital (formerly Gaon) chart are eligible to win. *Inkigayo* doesn't consider original soundtracks, variety show releases, songs unfit for broadcast (usually due to explicit language), or triple crown winners.

The criteria used to score candidates has a maximum of 11,000 points:

- Digital (*Melon, Genie, Bugs*): 50%, max 5,500 points
- Physical (Gaon/Circle Digital chart): 4.5%, max 500 points
- Social media (YouTube, Twitter, Weibo, YinYueTai): 31.8%, max 3,500 points
- Pre-vote (AZTalk app): 4.5%, max 500 points
- On air (playtime on SBS programs): 9%, max 1,000 points

International fans aren't allowed to participate in voting for *Inkigayo*, but they can help with streaming.

M Countdown

M Countdown wins are open to artists who are promoting their song on the day of the broadcast. Original soundtracks or triple crown winners are excluded.

The criteria used by *M Countdown* has a maximum of 11,000 points:

- Digital (*Mnet, Melon, Genie, Bugs*): 41%, max 4500 points
- Physical (Hanteo chart): 14%, max 1,500 points
- Social media (YouTube and *M Countdown* clips): 18%, max 2000 points
- Pre-vote (*Mnet* app): 9%, max 1,000 points
- Live vote (*Mnet* app): 9%, max 1,000 points
- Broadcast score: 9%, max 1,000 points

International fans can participate in both live and pre-voting through the *Mnet* app. Pre-voting starts each Friday before the broadcast at 2 p.m. KST and goes until the Monday before the broadcast at 9 a.m. KST. You can vote once daily during this period.

Music Bank

Music Bank allows competitors to earn a maximum of 200,000 points for songs, excluding original soundtracks or variety show releases.

Music Bank uses the following criteria to rank competitors:

- Digital: 65%, max 130,000 points
- 58.5% online, max 117,000 points (*Genie, Melon, Naver Music, Bugs, Soribada*)
- 6.5% mobile, max 13,000 points (downloads for ringtones)
- Physical (Hanteo chart)
- Broadcast score (playtime on KBS programs): 40,000 points
- 17% TV play
- 3% radio play
- Viewer panel survey: 10%, max 20,000 points

Fans can still stream to help with digital scores, but there's no direct fan voting for *Music Bank*. Korean fans may be randomly selected to participate in the viewer panel survey if they're registered for the KBS survey panel, but there's no guarantee of that opportunity.

Show Champion

On *Show Champion*, eligible songs that aren't triple crown winners or original soundtracks are ranked on a percentage basis.

The following criteria is used:

- Digital (Melon, Bugs, Genie, Soribada): 30%
- Physical: 10%
- Pre-vote (Idol Champ app and Genie website): 40%
- Expert score: 10%
- Broadcast score (playtime on MBC programs): 10%

Show Champion is one of the best shows for international fans, as they can participate in both the pre-vote and streaming, which are huge portions of the overall score.

The *Show Champion* pre-vote is divided into two parts, each of which makes up 20 percent of the total score. International fans can vote on the *Idol Champ* app and the *Genie* website. Voting begins the Tuesday eight days prior and ends the Sunday before the broadcast.

Show! Music Core

Show! Music Core uses a maximum of 10,000 points to score eligible entries. It excludes original soundtracks, variety show releases, unfit songs as determined by the network, songs older than three months, and pre-debut releases.

The division of the points is as follows:

- Digital: 50%, max 5,000 points
- Physical: 10%, max 1,000 points
- Video (YouTube): 10%, max 1,000 points
- Radio (MBC programs): 5%, max 500 points
- Live text vote: 15%, max 1,500 points
- Viewer panel survey: 10%, max 1000 points

Show! Music Core doesn't allow international fans to vote, so they must focus on streaming (including MVs) if they want to improve this score.

The Show

The Show allows Korean and international fans a chance to impact their idols' success through streaming and international voting.

On *The Show*, contestants who perform on broadcast day are eligible to earn up to 10,000 points:

- Digital sales: 40%, max 4,000 points
- Physical sales: 10%, max 1,000 points
- Video (YouTube views): 20%, max 2,000 points
- Expert score: 15%, max 1,500 points
- Pre-vote (on STARPASS app): 5%, max 500 points
- Live vote (on STARPASS app): 10%, max 1,000 points

Pre-voting for *The Show* starts the Friday before the show at 8 p.m. KST and ends 2 p.m. KST the Monday before broadcast. Fans around the world can cast their votes during this period, then again during the live show.

Simply K-Pop

Simply K-Pop focuses on playing and highlighting K-pop music rather than voting and streaming scores, so fans are less directly involved.

Music Universe K-909

The focus of *Music Universe K-909* isn't on ranking songs; rather, it's a platform for artists, particularly new artists, to showcase themselves. Segments are designed to create high-quality engagement and help fans get to know artists. Thus, fans don't do a lot for this music show.

FAN ART, FANFICTION, & FAN-MADE CONTENT

K-pop fans excel at creating content, including fanfiction, fan art, and video compilations. Fan-made content helps establish bonds between fans and encourages a deeper commitment to fan behaviors. A main component of K-pop is fantasies that fans have about their idols, and fan content brings those fantasies to life.

Fans make a range of content, and some of the most useful content introduces non-fans to idols. For example, videos of idols on TikTok commonly go viral, exposing new people to the K-pop world. Stunning visuals and humor are both great ways to draw in new fans. Primer videos and "get to know the idol" content also help potential fans learn more.

Social media is the predominant place to find this fan content, and most social media platforms have some level of fan interaction. X, Instagram, TikTok, and YouTube provide some of the biggest fan engagement.

Through fan-made content, fans get to showcase their creative abilities while also promoting their idols. This labor is crucial to companies looking to optimize their artists' global impact. From content creation to translation, fans help spread their artists' work in exciting and novel ways.

K-POP CONVENTIONS & EVENTS

The international success of K-pop means there are conventions and events designed for international lovers of K-pop. Events like KCON have become important to K-pop fans looking to find community and opportunities to see idols perform in person.

Since the beginning, there have always been K-pop festivals and events, even internationally. Areas like Los Angeles and New York have large populations of Korean immigrants, so they've always celebrated their roots. However, these events have grown even bigger and more diverse as new fans seek to find like-minded people and learn more about K-pop and its culture.

K-pop conventions include live performances from K-pop stars but also include other activities, food, and merchandise. When you're at a convention, you usually have special opportunities for interaction with idols like photo ops, hi-touch events, and fansigns. These often cost extra and include a lottery system.

Conventions provide a chance to spend time around something you enjoy, but you also get to meet other people. Talking to fellow fans or meeting online friends in person is one of the best parts of any convention, so don't be afraid to venture out of your comfort zone and get to know some of your fellow fans.

THE WORLD OF K-POP MERCHANDISING

Merchandise is a part of K-pop that you cannot miss, but it can be overwhelming to get started—there's so much to choose from! There are often multiple versions of the same album and tons of EPs to go along with the LPs. You may feel you have a lot of catching up to do, especially when you realize there are sometimes hundreds of photocards you can collect if your bias is already established.

Some examples of common K-pop merch include:

- Physical albums (CDs or vinyl)
- Photocards
- Postcards
- Photobooks
- Season's Greetings boxes (typically including a calendar/planner for the upcoming year, along with group-specific goodies)
- Light sticks
- Clothing and accessories
- Concert merch
- DVDs of live performances

If you want to create a collection of your own, start by making a list of items you want most. Do you already have a light stick? Are there certain photocards you want? Would you rather just focus on albums, then get everything else as you go?

No matter what your priorities are, it's important to plan so that you can look for items accordingly. There's plenty of time to get what you want, so don't feel like you have to rush. Take a deep breath and purchase items when you can.

To look for items, you can check out K-pop stores online or in person. You can also look on secondhand markets like eBay or fan trading forums. Fans often initiate photocard trades on social media, so you can look there too, but always do so with an abundance of caution.

All this stuff may seem endless, but remember: You don't need it all! Get what makes you feel satisfied. If you don't like photocards, don't get them just because everyone else does. If you love photo cards, that's cool too. Don't get ahead of yourself, and keep in mind that physical items aren't a requirement to be a fan. However, if you want to start a collection, you can do so at your own pace.

THE ROLE OF YOUTUBE & REACTION VIDEOS

K-pop music reaction channels are popular because fans love to see other fans' thoughts on their biases' comebacks and MVs. Reactions can create a wave of popularity for a song or idol or even make them go viral.

Fans watch reaction videos when they can, and increased views encourage the creator to make additional content for those artists in the future. Those reaction videos also help non-fans find the videos and pique their interest. Reaction channels have become more popular as the dynamic between fans and creators grows.

HOW TO GET INVOLVED IN K-POP DANCE COVERS

One way K-pop groups reach audiences is through dance challenges. These are particularly successful on platforms like TikTok that offer short form content. It's common for groups to start a challenge for new releases. Fans post videos of themselves dancing to a catchy part of the song, which draws new listeners in, especially if they hear it several times and it gets stuck in their heads.

If you want to get involved in K-pop dance covers, you don't actually need to be a great dancer. All you need to do is dance and learn. Artists usually choose relatively simple choreography to make it more accessible. In some cases, other fans make video guides to help you learn the dance. Making dance videos takes practice, but with a little effort, you'll be on your way to looking like a dance pro.

THE IMPORTANCE OF FANCAMS

Fancams are a great way to showcase the skills and visuals of individual idols because they each focus on just one member of a group or follow the dancing of a soloist. Fans enjoy watching their bias the entire performance without being distracted by the rest of the stage. While the main camera's purpose is to show the best of everything, fancams are designed to show specific groups of fans what they want to see.

In K-pop, fancams grew in popularity after a fancam of Hani from EXID performing "Up and Down" went viral in Korea. The song reentered Korean charts and reached number one, proving that fancams could do big things for artists. Other groups began hosting fancams too, not only creating domestic success but also appealing to global audiences. Accordingly, fancams provide an opportunity to highlight certain members and increase overall engagement and the odds of an idol going viral.

While the focus of fancams is the fans, they also have the power to boost the music and reach new audiences. Initially, fancams felt more personal, but they've since been commercialized. TV programs like Mnet's *M Countdown* began to release fancams of performance rehearsals online. These fancams have become one of the main things Mnet is known for among international audiences. As popularity of these fancams has grown, so has the broadcasters' commitment to providing YouTube content for fans.

While non-K-pop fandoms sometimes become frustrated with the spamming of K-pop fancams, these videos have become not just entertainment but also agents of change. After the death of George Floyd, K-pop fans spammed social media with fancams to prevent police from tracking protestors. They used Black Lives Matter hashtags to trend the tags higher and make it harder for police to find certain posts. Whether this strategy was helpful is debatable, but it demonstrates the long history of K-pop being used in conjunction with activism and to create social change.

INTERNATIONAL K-POP COLLABORATIONS

In recent years, it has become more common for K-pop artists to collaborate with international artists to cross promote and appeal to fans around the world. Collaborations are just another way of showing the world what K-pop is all about and why they should listen to it even if they aren't from Korea.

BLACKPINK has had several notable collaborations that helped make the group a global name. "Sour Candy" was a chance for BLACKPINK to join forces with mega-pop star Lady Gaga. The catchy song seamlessly merged pop and K-pop to create a song that didn't make either artist feel like an afterthought. Several BLACKPINK members have also had success with solo collabs. Rosé gained major traction with her Bruno Mars collaboration "Apt.," and Jennie joined forces with The Weeknd and Lily-Rose Depp in "One of the Girls."

There have been several major collaborations over the years. BTS's Jungkook made a splash with his 2023 all-English album *Golden*, which was full of collaborations and remixes with Western artists. His remix of "Standing Next to You" with Usher combined stunning vocals with smooth choreography, and the earworm "Seven" with Latto established itself as a summer anthem. With the help of English lyrics and well-known Western artists, Jungkook primed himself to gain Western attention.

International K-pop collaborations haven't just been focused on gaining Western attention for artists. "Social Path" by Stray Kids features Japanese singer LiSA, displaying an exciting collab between two well-respected artists. The song was a fitting choice for the Stray Kids Japanese album *Social Path / Super Bowl*, and their feature of a popular Japanese artist helped the group gain attention.

It's always exciting to see new collaborations, and with K-pop's dominance, global artists want a chance to work with K-pop stars. They know K-pop's strong fanbase can bring huge numbers to their songs. Thus, collaborations are mutually beneficial to all artists involved.

THE IMPACT OF K-POP ON THE GLOBAL MUSIC INDUSTRY

As you can see, when it comes to global appeal, K-pop has a strong foundation of blending cultures to create a large, diverse fanbase. However, K-pop has not only borrowed from other cultures — it's also influenced other cultures and the global music industry at large.

Perhaps the most obvious impact of K-pop on the global music industry is its influence on fan culture. While fandoms have obviously existed as long as fans themselves have, K-pop has demonstrated the power of a loyal and dedicated fanbase. K-pop also serves as a model of fan engagement, as most K-pop is generally more interactive than other genres.

For music around the globe, fan behavior has become more central in marketing. Some Western artists have even taken notes from K-pop stars' album packaging and started including photocards or other extras commonly provided within the genre. Live streams,

110

special editions, and streaming initiatives have become essential for fans who want their biases to succeed. Additionally, fans have started to create fancams for all types of content, not just K-pop.

Another example of K-pop's global impact comes from the use of survival shows. In recent years, global labels have teamed with K-pop labels in attempts to replicate the success of Korean survival shows. Music moguls like Simon Cowell have expressed the desire to create Western K-pop groups. The British group dearALICE was formed on the show *Made in Korea: The K-Pop Experience.* Participants traveled to Seoul to train and eventually debut as a Western group made with Korean methodologies.

K-pop's success has also helped spotlight other music markets. For example, the success of BLACKPINK's Lisa brought listeners' attention to Thai culture due to Lisa's Thai roots. Lisa has showcased Thai culture through her fashion and MVs; she has even made some Thai brands, such as Labubu, a toy company known for its push puppets. As a result of increased exposure to Thai culture, some K-pop fans started to listen to Thai pop as well.

Similarly, MiSaMo is a subunit composed of TWICE's Japanese members. The group debuted in 2023 and allows its members to release J-pop music under a Japanese label. Exposure to MiSaMo gave global audiences the chance to experience J-pop and, again, shows how interconnected the global music scene is.

While it's clear that K-pop has had a strong influence on global music, the genre has likewise had a profound impact on the international music scene. This dynamic will only continue to grow as K-pop continues to dominate as a major part of the global music scene.

CHAPTER SIX:
K-POP MUSIC & AWARDS

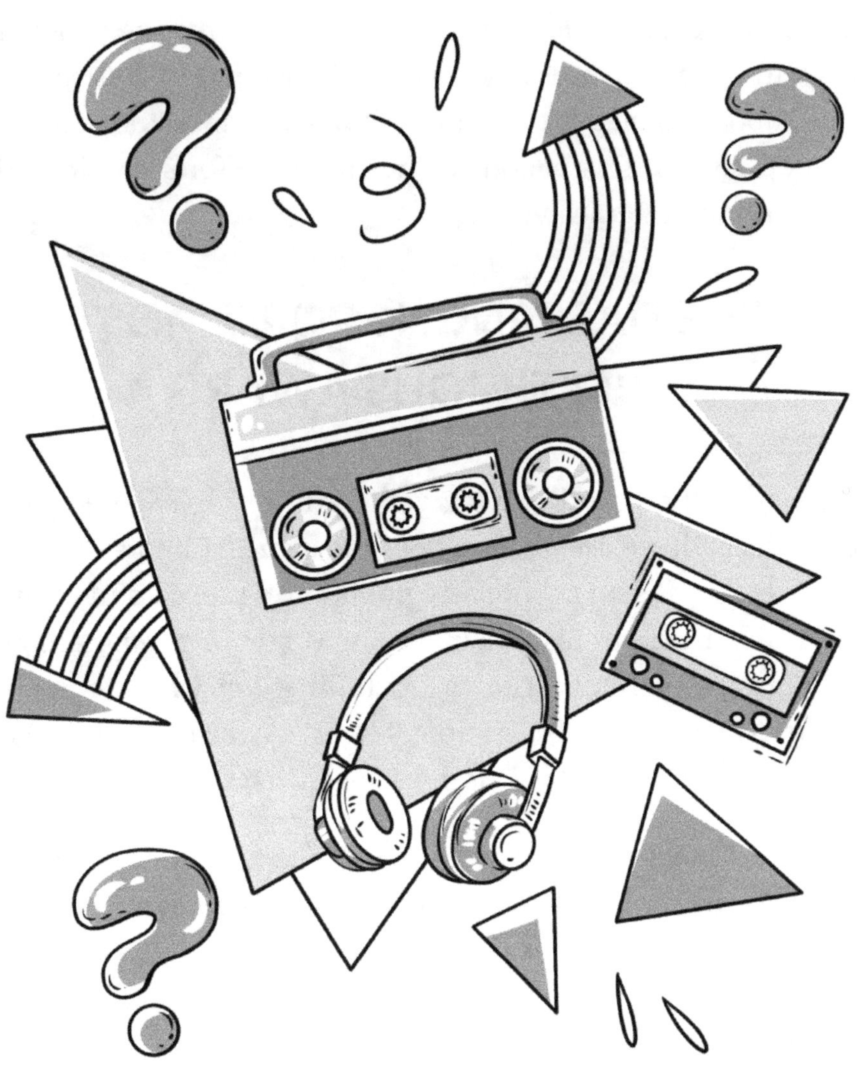

Before wrapping up our K-pop journey, it's time to examine the many achievements the genre has collected over the years. From exploring the role of award shows and the glory of the *daesang* to showcasing original soundtracks that defined movie scenes, K-pop is full of triumphs that fans can celebrate.

These accomplishments also help sustain the creative and artistic energy that make K-pop so vibrant and thrilling. Of course, K-pop isn't all about accolades or topping charts, but an acknowledgment of K-pop's success is a nod to the tireless efforts of idols, their teams, and their dedicated fans.

THE DAESANG: K-POP'S MOST PRESTIGIOUS AWARD

A *daesang* is the grand prize given during Korean music award shows. Receiving a *daesang* is one of the biggest honors that K-pop artists can get. It's an acknowledgment of the successful efforts of not just the artist but also their team and fans. *Daesangs* are given at a number of music shows, including the MAMA Awards, Korean Music Awards, Melon Music Awards, Genie Music Awards, Golden Disc Awards, and Fact Music Awards.

While the *daesang* is the grand prize, K-pop acts are also awarded *bonsang* awards, or a "main prize," which basically acknowledge the runners-up. *Bonsang* awards may not be as prestigious as *daesang* awards, but they're still a highly sought-after honor. From a Western perspective, it may help to think of the *daesang* like one of the Big Four Grammy Awards (Album of the Year, Record of the Year, Song of the Year, and Best New Artist).

Different award shows have different *daesang* categories and use their own parameters to determine the winner, generally based on sales figures and judge evaluations. Among the *daesang* awards, wins from shows like the Korean Music Awards, Seoul Music Awards, Golden Disc Awards, Melon Music Awards, and Mnet Asian Music Awards tend to be more prestigious than others.

The *daesang* awards aren't easy to get, but several artists have received huge numbers of these grand prizes over the course of their careers. BTS is famous for their success at award shows, with more than 70 *daesangs*, and its members have won prizes through their solo work.

EXO has also won a significant number of prizes and had earned the most *daesang* awards before BTS began its reign. TWICE is supreme among girl groups. Other notable figures with tons of grand prizes are BIGBANG, IU, PSY, Girls' Generation, H.O.T., g.o.d., 2NE1, and Super Junior.

THE BIGGEST K-POP MUSIC AWARD SHOWS

When it comes to award shows, it's important for K-pop fans to be familiar with the main ones. Some of these shows aren't as prestigious or anticipated by fans, but they all give K-pop stars the chance to win big prizes, and each is an honor to win. Most of these shows take place either toward the end or near the beginning of the year. Some prizes have fan voting, while others are entirely dependent on sales or judges' input.

MAMA Awards

The MAMA Awards, formerly known as the Mnet Asian Music Awards, are perhaps the most known by internation fans. These awards are considered highly prestigious for K-pop artists. Although the show honors artists in several Asian countries, most of the awards go to K-pop artists. The event was first held in 1999 and was modeled on the MTV Video Music Awards. It has since evolved to become more inclusive and expansive.

This show awards *daesangs* in four categories: Artist of the Year, Album of the Year, Song of the Year, and Worldwide Icon of the Year. Other awards include Best Group (Male and Female), Best Artist (Male and Female), Best Music Video, Best Original Soundtrack, and Best Performance (Rap, Vocal, and Dance). In addition to these, special awards like Best Asian Artist or Best International Artist may be given out.

Golden Disc Awards

The Golden Disc Awards was created in 1986 as the Korea Visual and Records Grand Prize Award before being revamped in 2015. The award was originally created to honor various pop culture achievements and encourage a thriving Korean pop culture scene.

The Golden Disc Awards offers two *daesangs*: Album of the Year and Song of the Year. It also offers additional prizes, including the Album *Bonsang*, Digital Song *Bonsang*, Rookie Artist Award, and more.

Korean Music Awards

The Korean Music Awards are some of the most highly anticipated domestic award shows, and while many of the awards go to K-pop idols, categories include a range of genres. The show first aired in 2004, and while it has evolved over time, it remains highly prestigious. It stands out as a show that gives prizes based on a panel of expert judges.

The KMAs has three *daesangs*: Song of the Year, Album of the Year, and Musician of the Year. Twenty prizes are given in different genre categories, and additional awards include Rookie of the Year, popularity awards, and special choice committee awards.

Melon Music Awards

The Melon Music Awards is Kakao Entertainment's award show. It started in 2005 as a fan-voted award show held purely online, but in 2009, it began to develop into one of South Korea's major in-person award shows. The Melon Music Awards uses the Melon Music platform's data, voting, and judges' scores to determine the winners.

Fans can participate in Melon Music Awards, as most categories have some level of fan voting (excluding special awards, which are determined entirely by the judges). For *daesang, bonsangs,* and Best New Artist, 20 percent is based on the judges' score, 20 percent on online voting, and 60 percent on digital sales. For genre awards, 30 percent is based on the judges' score, 30 percent on online voting, and 40 on percent digital sales. Finally, popularity awards are 60 percent online voting and 40 percent digital sales.

The Melon Music Awards has four *daesangs:* Artist of the Year, Song of the Year, Album of the Year, and Record of the Year. The show also includes genre awards in various categories that include artists from K-pop and beyond. Popularity prizes include the Netizen's Choice Award and the Hot Trend Award.

Seoul Music Awards

The Seoul Music Awards, presented by the newspaper *Sports Seoul*, began in 1990. It combines sales, judges' votes, and the popular vote to determine winners. Although the focus is largely on K-pop, other genres are included as well.

While this show awards multiple *bonsangs*, only one act receives a *daesang*. However, exceptions occurred at the ninth and tenth shows when two artists shared the grand prize, and the twenty-ninth ceremony when *daesangs* were awarded in both album and digital categories.

Other prizes include the K-Wave Special Award, chosen by international voters, and the Popularity Award, selected by domestic audiences. Other awards include New Artists Award, Best Album, Best Song, and genre-specific awards.

Genie Music Awards

The Genie Music Awards is a relatively new music show organized using Genie Music's chart data combined with online voting and judges' voting. This show only began in 2022, so its influence remains limited.

Three *daesangs* are awarded in the categories of Top Artist, Top Album, and Top Music. It also gives awards for best male and female groups, best male and female artists, and Best New Artist, along with genre-specific prizes.

The Fact Music Awards

The Fact Music Awards, or TMA, is another example of a fairly young music awards show. It was established in 2019 with awards based on Circle Chart data, a panel of judges, and both domestic and international fan participation.

This show features one *daesang*, given to an outstanding artist, but it also rewards *bonsangs* to runners-up. Other awards include Best Performer, Worldwide Icon, and Next Leader, along with a popularity award.

Hanteo Music Awards

The Hanteo Music Awards uses the Hanteo chart, fan voting, and various other criteria to determine winners in a range of categories, but it primarily uses chart data to recognize the top performers of the year.

The award show gives four *daesangs* in the following categories: Best Album, Best Artist, Best Song, and Best Performance. It also gives *bonsangs* for artist of the year, and other prizes include the Post Generation Award, Emerging Artist Award, Global Artist Award, and Rookie of the Year Award.

Circle Chart Music Awards

The Circle Chart Music Awards began as the Gaon Chart Music Awards in 2012 to give awards based on artists' performance on the Charts. The show has recently revamped its format; it used to give prizes based on sales per month or quarter, but since 2023, has chosen winners based on the entire year. Occasionally, these categories are further broken down by global streaming, digital sales, and unique listeners. Several acts are selected per category.

Korean Grand Music Awards

The Korean Grand Music Awards is a newer show that honors musicians across various genres—including, of course, K-pop. This awards show was established by the newspaper *Illgan Sports*, which previously created the Golden Disc Awards.

This show awards five *daesangs*: Grand Record, Grand Artist, Grand Song, Grand Performer, and Grand Honor's Choice. Other awards include *bonsangs* for Best Artist, Best Song, rookie awards, and genre categories.

THE IMPORTANCE OF FAN VOTING

Many award shows take fan voting into account as at least part of the criteria for winning; thus, fans who want their groups to succeed must be ready to do their part. As you might expect, the primary voter-oriented awards are typically in popularity categories.

Some award shows open their votes to international audiences, while others are limited to domestic votes, and each show uses a preferred app to vote. When in doubt, look to fanbases to see what you can do to help. Voting can get pretty hectic, but once you get in the swing of things, it isn't so bad.

CHART-TOPPING K-POP SONGS & RECORD-BREAKING ACHIEVEMENTS

Many K-pop songs, albums, and groups have topped the charts and broken records, paving the way for future K-pop artists. While it would be nearly impossible to list every achievement and success K-pop artists have attained, here are some of the main ones any fan should know.

BTS

More than any other group, BTS stands out for setting records left and right with chart-topping songs both domestically and abroad. Their popularity is almost impossible to fathom; BTS holds more than 20 Guinness World Records, proving that the K-pop genre can compete with the best of the world—not just the best of Korea. They distinguished themselves as the first Korean group to gain quintuple platinum certification and became the first K-pop act to top the Billboard charts with "Dynamite," which earned them a Grammy nomination.

BTS broke barrier after barrier to show the power of K-pop and establish themselves as a household name. As the best-selling Korean musical act of all time, the group has achieved four number-one singles in the United States and dominated Korean charts as well. In 2019, the group was named in *Time's* 100 list of most influential people in the world. The group's global impact may be surprising, but it's well earned.

BTS's success in Korea is not to be ignored either. The group holds more *daesangs* than any other act in history. For their role in spreading Korean culture, they were awarded the Order of Cultural Merit in South Korea—the youngest people ever to receive it. Since BTS's members have become some of the most famous representatives of Korea and Korean culture, the weight on their shoulders is huge.

BTS's individual members have also found success in solo careers, demonstrating their longevity and talent both as a whole and individually. There's no doubt that BTS will remain some of the most-decorated K-pop artists of all time and a source of national pride and inspiration.

IU

If you're looking for an outstanding soloist in K-pop, IU should come to mind. Songs like "Good Day" are considered some of the best K-pop songs ever made. In K-pop, soloists don't often get as much attention as groups, but IU earned a place as Korea's "little sister." This nickname shows the deep affection K-pop listeners have for the talented singer's soaring vocals, which have established her as an icon in K-pop. It's no wonder that IU stands out for having 21 songs achieve PAK status.

PSY

When it comes to chart-topping success, you can't leave out PSY's "Gangnam Style," which remains the most-viewed K-pop song on YouTube. It also received extensive radio and TV play in 2012, when it first went viral. PSY made a name for himself and gained unprecedented levels of exposure for K-pop.

Girls' Generation

Girls' Generation may not be as universally known as some of the other K-pop acts on this list, but this group was no doubt transformative for K-pop. In fact, *Rolling Stone* listed the song "Gee" as the greatest K-pop song of all time, describing it as "a pure distillation of the giddiness of infatuation."

BLACKPINK

Many iconic BLACKPINK songs have topped the charts and been among the most-viewed videos on YouTube. "DDU-DU DDU-DU" is not only the group's most-viewed video but also the first video by a Korean group to surpass both one and two billion views. "Kill This Love" also has more than two billion views, while "BOOMBAYAH," "How You Like That," and "As If It's Your Last" have all passed the one-billion-view mark.

Even BLACKPINK's dance practice videos have been huge, and the "How You Like That" dance practice video became the first to surpass one billion views. Now, the video has more than one and a half billion views, establishing it as one of the most successful dance practice videos ever.

The group has made a name for itself as one of the biggest girl groups ever, and members continue their huge success through solo work. This group proved Korean girl groups can compete in music markets worldwide, even becoming the first female Korean group to debut on the Billboard Emerging Artists Chart.

BLACKPINK was also the first Asian act to headline at Coachella. As if that wasn't enough, they're the first — and only — K-pop girl group to appear in Spotify's Billions Club by getting more than a billion streams for "How You Like That." The group remains a revolutionary one.

Stray Kids

As a fourth-generation group, Stray Kids debuted into a world with more awareness of K-pop than ever before; despite this, they had to fight to find success, demonstrating that K-pop idols still have boundaries to break. The group has proven itself as fourth-generation leader and highlights what K-pop fans can look forward to when it comes to K-pop's global influence.

Stray Kids made waves with achievements like performing at Lollapalooza, attending the Met Gala as a group, and selling out stadiums around the world. For its efforts, the group became the first fourth-generation K-pop group to receive a Commendation from the Prime Minister at the Korean Popular Culture and Arts Awards. At the time, only six other groups were given the award.

In 2024, Stray Kids became the first group ever to debut their first five chart entries at number one on the Billboard 200 Albums Chart with the release of the album *ATE*. Clearly, the future is bright for K-pop as each generation builds upon the work of the groups and idols who have come before.

HIDDEN GEMS: UNDERRATED K-POP TRACKS

For every chart-topper, there's a hidden gem that K-pop fans should know. These songs may not be the most popular, but that doesn't mean they aren't worth discovering. Some might call the artists behind these songs *nugus*, but they're still interesting if you enjoy diverse sounds and quality music.

"Congratulations" by DAY6

While JYP Entertainment may be known for groups like Stray Kids and TWICE, DAY6 is a group that excels at ballads and anthems alike. Members even play their own instruments, which makes DAY6 feel more like a band than an idol group. If you want a song full of cathartic angst, "Congratulations" is a great example of the depth this group brings to their music.

"Show Must Go On" by ONF

ONF is a six-member group that relies on sci-fi visuals to set themselves apart from other groups. "Show Must Go On" is a prime example of the group's catchy beats and eclectic sound. While the music stands on its own, sleek visuals and smooth choreography help tell the story of ONF's music.

"Chase Me" by Dreamcatcher

Dreamcatcher stays true to their name by creating songs with a dreamy but darkly mysterious feel. "Chase Me" showcases the girl group's use of genres like EDM, metal, and heavy rock. If you want something with an edge, "Chase Me" and other songs by Dreamcatcher will likely give you what you want.

"Candy (so good)" by The Rose

If you're looking for a group that cares deeply about instrumentation, The Rose's members play instruments and bring a rock feel to K-pop. "Candy (so good)" blends Korean and English lyrics to create a nice acoustic sound. More like a rock band than a traditional K-pop group, The Rose has a unique sound and shows how diverse K-pop can be.

"Hip" by MAMAMOO

MAMAMOO formed in 2014, and throughout their career, the group has pushed themselves to cross genres, creating music that challenges the norms of K-pop. The group is known for including amazing harmonies and other vocal achievements in songs like "Hip."

"5TAR (Incompletion)" by A.C.E

A.C.E stands out because the group has range when it comes to both vocal skills and dancing. With dynamic choreography and smooth vocal technique, songs like "5TAR (Incompletion)" demonstrate how the group pushes each members' abilities as they strive to create unique music that's distinct from any other group.

"Missing You" by BTOB

BTOB's "Missing You" has a slower tempo than a lot of K-pop songs while still managing to be super catchy. This change of pace shows that, although most K-pop may focus on faster songs, down-tempo songs still have a place in K-pop and can be a nice change of pace.

"So What" by LOONA

If you want a track that will get you on your feet, LOONA's "So What" will make you want to dance along. LOONA has some of the best choreography in the business yet maintains a unique concept. The group is currently on hiatus, but they've got tons of songs, so you can go digging for other hidden gems in their discography.

K-POP SOUNDTRACKS

Original soundtracks (OSTs) are an important part of the Korean music industry. While OSTs aren't the focus of K-pop, many K-pop stars participate in the creation of OSTs for K-dramas, anime, and movies. Entire groups may work on OSTs, but in many cases, K-pop idols work as soloists on OST projects, sometimes with other artists they wouldn't normally work with.

"Love You with All My Heart" by Crush

K-pop soloist Crush released "Love You with All My Heart" for the K-drama *Queen of Hearts*, and the song quickly became one of the most memorable tracks of 2024. It even won the MAMA award for Best OST.

"I'm in the Mood for Dancing" by Yuju

Yuju brought energy to the drama *True Beauty* with "I'm in the Mood for Dancing," which expertly reflects the coming-of-age theme of the show while utilizing the drumbeat to create a powerful mood.

"Eyes, Nose, Lips" by Taeyang

The drama *It's Okay, That's Love* released in 2014 and garnered attention for its portrayal of mental health struggles. To bring this drama to life, songs like "Eyes, Nose, Lips" by Taeyang were included in the soundtrack, capturing the characters' emotional turbulence and eventual healing. The song also made an appearance in *King the Land*, though it isn't included in that show's OST.

"Future" by Red Velvet

Red Velvet wowed fans with "Future," their track from the OST for *Start-Up*. The song is incredibly sweet and brings a hopeful and youthful energy to the show. The song definitely elicits swooning from listeners.

"Stay with Me" by Chanyeol (EXO) and Punch

EXO member Chanyeol teamed up with OST queen Punch to create one of the most memorable OSTs for *Goblin*, a supernatural love story with a soundtrack that evokes yearning and love.

"You Are My Everything" by Gummy

If you're looking for a ballad with big vocals and intense lyrics, "You Are My Everything" was used in *Descendants of the Sun* to capture the emotional intensity of the show and the characters' relationship. It's no wonder this song became a chart-topper, establishing Gummy as an artist to watch out for.

"Give You My Heart" by IU

Combine one of the most beloved K-pop soloists with one of the most popular K-dramas of all time, and you've got IU's "Give You My Heart." The track stands out as a lyrical tour de force that emphasizes the complex feelings characters dealt with in the drama *Crash Landing on You*.

"Orbit" by MAMAMOO's Hwasa

Hwasa's voice is perfect in *The King: Eternal Monarch,* a story about a couple split between two worlds who must confront personal hardships while under enormous pressure. "Orbit" adds depth and emotion to the story as a thoughtful and vocally strong OST.

K-POP ALBUMS: CONCEPTS & STORYTELLING

Concepts are huge part of K-pop albums and singles, driving the content with storytelling and overarching themes. A strong concept allows groups to showcase their skills and easily show fans what to expect from a comeback. Several iconic concepts will go down in K-pop history for standing out as stellar examples of theme and storytelling.

Gasoline by Key

SHINee's Key has always liked a strong concept in his solo work. He tends to go for maximalist images and vibrant colors. He also pushes the type of packing he uses for physical copies of the album to reiterate the tone of the songs. His second mini-album, *Gasoline,* is no exception and shows that Key always has his foot on the gas when it comes to concepts.

Map of the Soul: 7 by BTS

While BTS is known for having many memorable concepts, among the best is the concept of *Map of the Soul: 7*. The album was even chosen as one of *Rolling Stone's* 50 Greatest Concept Albums of All Time for its exploration of what it means to be idols who want to show their true selves while struggling against public perception and stage personas.

Kai by Kai

EXO's Kai made a splash when he released a vibrant concept for his self-titled solo album. The images are electric and show the bold direction that Kai intended to take with his first solo album.

Savage by aespa

Savage was aespa's first EP, and its bold concept certainly made an impression. The album's concept intended to show a sophisticated and modern side of aespa, demonstrating the group's desire to create content with substance and focus on quality music without any filler songs. The concept involved dark, futuristic themes and images of the members as machines, highlighting society's growing dependence on technology.

CONCLUSION:
YOUR K-POP JOURNEY: STAYING INVOLVED

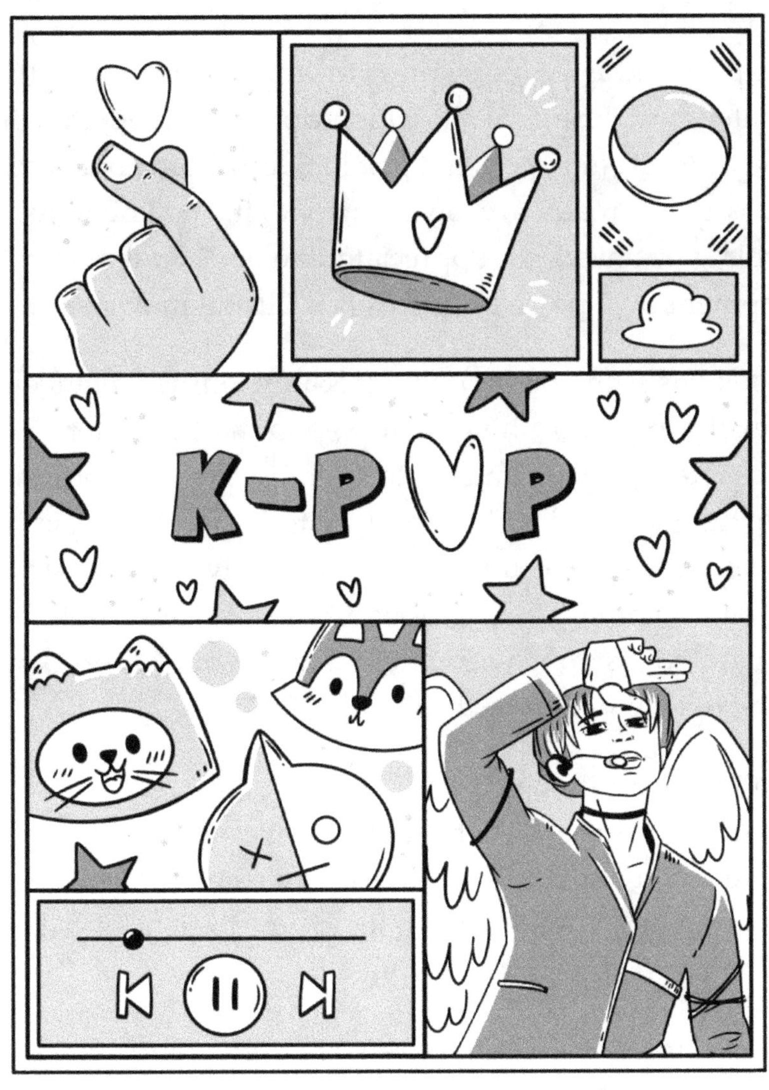

If you're a fan of pop culture, you've no doubt heard of K-pop before! As this book comes to a close, you've gotten an inside look at its inner workings. Whether you plan to become a fan or you just wanted to learn what K-pop is all about, you're now prepared to talk about K-pop when it comes up in conversation—and chances are, it will.

The K-pop industry continues to thrive, and by 2031, it's anticipated to become a $20-billion-dollar market, showing the growing interest in K-pop, not just in South Korea but around the world. You'll be ready to grow along with it, and you now have all the tools you need to appreciate the excitement and future development of K-pop as a genre and cultural movement.

This book has seen you off on your K-pop journey, but feel free to keep exploring everything that K-pop has to offer. To fully embrace K-pop, you must start embracing opportunities to participate. That can involve simply listening to the music, but you may want to include additional fan behaviors like streaming, voting, and joining K-pop groups. There's no one "right" way to participate, so it's up to you to define what your K-pop experience will look like going forward.

As you get more involved with K-pop, your tastes and interests may evolve, and that's part of what makes K-pop so wonderful. Your interest in K-pop can grow with you, and while it takes time to discover what you like, it's a lot of fun to figure it all out and meet a lot of great people along the way.

Above all, don't worry about remembering every detail. If you ever need a refresher on what something means or how something works, you can always come back to this book as a reference or share it with friends who may be interested in learning more. Now, empowered with all the things every K-pop fan should know, it's time to sit back or get up to dance and enjoy K-pop!

www.ingramcontent.com/pod-product-compliance
Lightning Source LLC
Chambersburg PA
CBHW060939050726
47592CB00003B/1025

9 781951 806866